S0-CAB-891

BARNES ON CREDIT AND COLLECTION

Every man who knows how to read has it in his power to magnify himself, to multiply the ways in which he exists, to make his life full, significant and interesting.

—Aldous Huxley

BARNES ON CREDIT AND COLLECTION

by

E. H. Barnes, Ph.D.

Vice President,
National Accounts System, Inc.

PRENTICE-HALL, INC.
Englewood Cliffs, N. J.

LIBRARY OF CONGRESS
CATALOG CARD NUMBER: 61-14578

First printing ....August, 1961
Second printing ....September, 1961

PRINTED IN THE UNITED STATES OF AMERICA
05588—MO

PREFACE

This book deals exclusively with consumer credit. It is intended to help those who grant credit to individuals for goods and for services and who have difficulty in collecting. The focus throughout is on collection, and credit is discussed only to the extent that such discussion is necessary to make clear the material on collection. It makes no pretense at being encyclopedic in its coverage of the topic, nor does it claim complete originality.

What is novel in the treatment is primarily the viewpoint, that of a psychologist who has embraced collection as his field. Sociological and psychological concepts are used to explain some of the phenomena of credit and collection in the hope that these concepts will provide new insights for the reader.

It was the need of the smaller credit granter for help in collection which originally prompted the writing of this book. Although it is hoped that the larger credit granter will also find ideas and suggestions of value, it is the smaller business and professional man to whom my remarks are primarily addressed. The larger credit granter can afford to employ credit experts and to maintain specialized departments to protect his rights and to promote the payment of his accounts. The smaller one must either do it himself or train others to do it for him.

Also, since the smaller credit granter is less likely to be concerned with installment credit, revolving credit, and the other complex forms, most of the text deals with the ordinary open account. The principles of collection, I feel, are basically similar for all accounts. They should, therefore, be applicable to the more highly developed plans as well. However, I have seldom made the attempt to illustrate these more complex applications specifically.

I do not expect everyone to agree with the viewpoints I have expressed. Indeed, I rather anticipate that some of the positions I have taken will be controversial if not downright unpopular. They are, however, my opinions at the present. Although I am indebted to many persons, I must take the responsibility for the views expressed.

Among those to whom I am indebted, I must first name my wife, Dr. Katharine Barnes, not only for intellectual stimulation and criticism, but also for her long hours of clerical assistance. Gordon Fletcher, president of National Accounts System, first interested me in the field of collection and has since been the source of a number of my ideas. Thanks certainly are due James Koller, Roland Gembala, Arnold Agnos, Joseph Savard, Gil Hamblet, Avis Fletcher, and Carl Hobbett for their help in such matters as reading the manuscript and offering valuable criticism and advice. Elsie Katterjohn and Katharine Fay have earned my gratitude through editorial help and proof reading.

TABLE OF CONTENTS

THE CREDIT DILEMMA

I

THE CREDIT DILEMMA

Each year those who grant credit are bilked of money running into hundreds of millions of dollars because debtors fail to honor their obligations. Yet, not only do these credit granters continue to extend credit, they actually expand their credit operations. In the face of staggering credit losses our economy is experiencing a soaring increase in the use of consumer credit. From seven billion dollars in 1939, to 16 billion in 1949, to 50 billion by the end of 1959, consumer credit today continues its rocketing rise. It would appear, on the surface, to be a paradox that the traditionally shrewd American businessman not only takes such losses, but actually seems to seek them.

The explanation of the paradox is, of course, that credit operations can be made profitable despite inevitable losses. It is a fact that the granting of credit can increase sales. People find it easier to buy when they use credit, and they buy more. Even a laboratory animal will go to be fed more frequently if he has to endure a slight shock some time *after* each feeding than he will if the shock is experienced just *before* feeding. So, too, human beings find it easier to have their needs satisfied now and take the shocks later. Since credit sales are based on such a fundamental and primitive principle of behavior, it is unlikely that the trend toward credit buying will spontaneously change.

Loss of Capital or Loss of Profits?

The credit granter, then, expects the increase in sales to result in profits which compensate him for the loss he suffers in bad debts. The modern businessman who deals on a credit basis should be taking an attitude similar to that of the insurance company, or the poker player. He should be deliberately taking a calculated risk and should expect to take occasional losses. If he has no losses, he is playing the game too close to the belt and is missing opportunities for profit. On the other hand, if he has too many losses, he may quickly find his stack of chips melting away, and soon he is out of the game. He is constantly faced with a choice between two risks. He may fail to gain a possible profit through being too selective or he may lose capital through taking too great a chance.

Since there is no perfectly reliable measure of credit risk, no sure-fire way of predicting how individuals will behave, the dilemma of the credit granter is made difficult by the relationship between these two risks. Diminishing either risk automatically increases the other. It is not possible to minimize both risks simultaneously. If the credit granter pursues a "tight credit" policy, he will inevitably sacrifice some business which would have been profitable. On the other hand, if he relaxes his standards and pursues a more liberal policy, he will certainly increase his loss from bad debt. There is no course which is free of both risks if credit is granted. The credit granter must choose which risk he desires to minimize.

There are businessmen who take extreme attitudes toward each of these two risks. The tightest of credit policies is, of course, represented by those who refuse to deal on credit, those who keep all transactions on a strictly cash basis. These persons, in a credit sense, are the ultimate conservatives. Often they thrive by advertising that they can cut costs by not dealing on credit and so are able to pass savings along to their customers. Of course, the large scale credit granter retaliates by pointing out that his large volume makes it possible to sell with a low mark-up plus the savings made possible by volume purchasing. The smaller credit granter stresses convenience.

The other extreme is represented by those who grant credit almost indiscriminately to virtually anyone who wants to buy. Since these individuals, consciously or not, are choosing to maximize the potentially more dangerous of the two risks, they must strive in every way to protect themselves from possible consequences. This they do, mainly, in two ways. First, they take advantage of every legal safeguard available. Examples of these safeguards include such devices as judgment notes and wage assignments. Second, they unblushingly pass their credit losses along to their more responsible customers. They do this in a variety of ways which is limited only by the ingenuity of their management. Increased carrying charges are only one of the more unimaginative means.

Responsibility of Credit Granters

It is not possible to pass by a discussion of this kind of unbridled risk-taking without including a few words of sermonizing. Beyond the moral issues concerning the responsibility a businessman owes to his society, his fellow businessmen, or to his less fortunate brothers, there are reasons for objecting to such practices on economic and more selfish grounds.

Whether the credit granter is ethically obligated to determine whether a new debt would overburden a prospective customer is, perhaps, a debatable question. Nevertheless, the public will insist that he share the responsibility for the individual unhappiness and personal tragedies which result from unrestrained credit buying. Whether the responsibility for being financially prudent belongs solely to the individual or not, society has traditionally insisted that its less capable members be protected, either from temptations which they cannot resist or from the consequences of yielding to those temptations. The laws relating to child labor and to bankruptcy are only two instances of the effects of this insistence, among a number which could be cited. In numerous cases public sentiment against exploitation of individual weaknesses has been crystallized into law. The unfortunate will always have their champions and their defenders.

Unless credit granters assume a portion of the burden for controlling the granting of credit, they will invite compulsory regulations. Public sympathy is normally on the side of the individual rather than the company, and American sentiment characteristically is for the unfortunate. Compulsory regulation, therefore, is likely to be restrictive, if not actually punitive. The businessman with foresight will voluntarily assume more responsibility for protecting the credit buyer against over-extending himself, and he will encourage others to do likewise.

Reciprocal Relationship of Risks

Fortunately, most credit granters do take a position between these two extremes. They neither refuse to deal on credit, nor do they grant credit indiscriminately. They grant credit to selected individuals only. However, it seems that most credit granters are overly impressed with the more obvious risk, that of loss of capital. Seldom are credit policies based on a clear and conscious understanding of both risks, the relationship between the two, and a deliberate choice of the weights to be assigned to each.

The small credit granter frequently does not really expect to take any credit loss. He finds it difficult to accept the fact that human frailty is as much a fact of life as the weather. Credit granting is risk-taking. One cannot be right all the time, and losses, over the long term, are inevitable. The small credit granter often finds it difficult to view credit losses as a natural consequence of credit business, something to be minimized rather than eliminated. He resents them and struggles to recoup. Like the inexperienced poker player, he often throws good money after bad in an effort to salvage something from a bad bet.

The larger credit granter is more sophisticated in some ways; he expects to take a loss. Nevertheless, he keeps a careful eye on the loss ratio and notes any increase with alarm. Such an increase is a signal for more careful screening of credit applicants, more rigorous follow-up of past due accounts, and a general tightening of controls. Then, when profits slip, the word goes out to be more liberal. This attitude reveals an implicit belief that both risks may be minimized simultaneously, and this cannot be done.

Liberalizing the extension of credit without taking more losses is like decanting more clear water from a partly settled muddy mixture; as you come closer to the bottom of the container you pour off more of the sediment.

If there were some sharp line which could be drawn between the gilt-edged credit risk and the poor one, it would be possible to bring both risks to a minimum level at the same time. But, like the muddy water, there is the hazy middle area which includes both elements. As you liberalize, you get more bad credit risks along with the good. It is merely a question of the degree of dilution you can tolerate.

Factors Influencing Credit Policy

Part of this vacillation in credit policy may stem from a fundamental change in the character of credit granting which has not been reflected in the typical accounting procedures. The use of consumer credit has been showing its phenomenal expansion precisely because it stimulates sales. Credit is being used more and more as a marketing tool, but it continues to be treated as a separate expense item rather than being viewed as a part of the cost of sales. Thus, the effect of changes in credit policy on the total profitability of an operation cannot be easily evaluated from the usual financial reports. Decisions concerning credit policy continue to be made primarily on the basis of loss ratios.

Loss ratios tell only part of the story. They reflect only the success or lack of success achieved in avoiding loss of capital. The performance of your credit policy in generating more profits is missing from the scene.

Demand and supply

In deciding on a credit policy, current conditions of demand and supply should play an important role. Perhaps a concrete example will make this clear. A large utility company finds itself with a heavy investment in idle expensive plant and equipment located in an economically depressed area where the majority of the residents appear to be marginal credit risks. Such a situation is one which weighs heavily in the direction of liberalizing credit policy. The company is already suffering major losses in depreciation and obsolescence while facilities stand idle. The credit loss from risking increased utilization of the plant and equipment may possibly be sustained and still result in an over-all increase in profitability. A decision to liberalize policy, however, cannot be made intelligently unless credit losses are placed in proper perspective, unless accounting reports yield the kind of data on which such a decision can be made. Loss ratios are not enough.

Cost of money

Certainly the availability and the cost of capital for investment in accounts receivable is a factor to be considered in fixing credit policy. When capital is expensive or scarce, this fact should weigh in the direction of tighter credit. Many a businessman has foundered because he failed to realize that a credit operation necessitates carrying a more or less permanent investment in accounts receivable just as he does in furniture and fixtures. Although accounts receivable may be carried as current assets, they are current only in a limited sense. As each account is liquidated it should be replaced by another. The total may shrink or expand, but a certain minimum, in a going credit business, is permanent investment. The cost of this investment should be considered in relation to its yield. Again, the cost cannot be compared to the yield unless the yield is known.

Cost of collection

Since an account receivable is created for the sole purpose of being liquidated, the cost of achieving this liquidation is another factor to be considered in establishing credit policy. Each time a dollar makes a trip from inventory, to accounts receivable, to cash, and back to inventory again, it should generate a profit. The collection effort is one of the pumps producing this cash flow and the cost of operating the pump is a critical factor in credit policy. Liberalizing credit increases the costs of collection as well as increasing direct credit losses. As greater risks are taken in granting credit, the proportion of delinquent accounts rises together with higher costs in billing and handling. It is strangely rare to find these costs separated from the costs of granting credit in most firms. Few companies actually know how much they spend on collection itself. As a result they may well lose control of collection costs and make uneconomic efforts at recovery.

An intelligently conducted credit operation can be the source of increased profits, as many thousands of businessmen have discovered. Operating a credit business, though, has perils which cannot be eliminated. The credit granter is forever in a dilemma, caught between the reciprocal dangers of losing capital and of losing potential profits. If he is to steer the best course between these two shoals, he needs information on the costs of collection, the effects of changes in credit policy on total profitability, conditions of demand and supply, the cost of money, and credit losses. He should be able to view his credit operations in proper relation to his total marketing effort. His credit policy should be flexible enough to permit him to change course as these factors vary.

OBTAINING CREDIT INFORMATION

II

OBTAINING CREDIT INFORMATION

Credit is merely an intermediate step in the process of receiving money from sales. It is this process—converting goods and services to money, siphoning some of the money off as profit, and returning the remainder to the cycle—which constitutes the basic activity of most business. Credit is expected to increase the volume of this flow but not to dam it up. Seen in this perspective, collection is the goal of all credit granting and, therefore, collection actually begins with credit granting. An account which has been opened properly is already well on its way to liquidation. Conversely, the seeds of later credit loss are often planted at the same time.

An intelligent approach to the granting of credit does not seek to eliminate all risk, but rather seeks a profitable balance between risks. It keeps in mind the reciprocal relationship between the two basic risks, loss of potential profit and loss of capital.

In trying to steer an optimum course between the two perils, the wise credit man will not forget that most credit granters have a rather strong bias to avoid more carefully the risk of loss of capital. It is somehow easier to tolerate the loss of what one might have had than the loss of something one already has had. The write-off of bad debts is a painful experience to most businessmen because it represents a junking of assets, throwing money away. Since potential profits were never on the books, these might-have-been assets can be dismissed more lightly, and failure to realize them can be rationalized away.

This, of course, is a conservative attitude and is, to a reasonable extent, realistic. A continuous loss of capital can result in failure of the business, while one can continue in business indefinitely without realizing maximum returns. Gambling for potential gains runs counter to this conservative attitude. However, it is important to realize that the business which embraces credit has already partially abandoned conservatism and should have done so with its eyes open to the less conservative position it has taken. The primary reason for accepting the risks of a credit operation lies in the possibility of increased profits. One should not allow a bias toward conservatism to cheat him of these potential gains.

To whichever side the credit granter wishes to lean in his risk taking, the evaluation of that risk begins with the opening of an account. To the more sophisticated credit man, it may seem unnecessary to point out that a credit application should be obtained before credit is extended. Yet, it is a fact that some credit granters do not obtain credit applications, and even more obtain very inadequate information. Of course, the question of what constitutes adequate credit information is a debatable one and the answer may well vary from business to business. Nevertheless, there is a consensus about general areas of inquiry and the meaning of some of the information which can be obtained.

Uses of Credit Information—The Three "E's"

Estimation of risk

Perhaps some of the disagreement about the credit information which should be obtained stems from the fact that credit information has several uses. The first use, and the most obvious one, is to provide a basis for estimating the risk involved in opening an account. Since this is the primary use of credit information, it receives the most attention. Such items as credit references, bank accounts, home ownership, and income level are included in the inquiry to provide a basis for judging the character of the credit applicant, his capacity to earn, and his capital resources. These three, character, capacity, and capital, are the traditional three C's on which evaluations of credit risk are usually made.

Enforcing collection

There is another use for credit information which is often neglected at the time the original application is taken. Information may be needed to provide a point of departure for later collection efforts in the event that the account goes bad. Such items as full name, previous addresses, employer's name and address, and the name of spouse are among those items which are important for this purpose. Personal references, though they may never be checked when estimating risk, can be very helpful in locating the customer who has decamped without paying.

Evaluating results

Further, credit information should be used for research purposes. It ought to provide a source of information about the accuracy of past decisions. It should be possible to compare the records of those who proved to be bad credit risks with those who proved to be good. Comparisons of this kind can reveal sources of error in your credit granting procedures. Research on the accuracy of past credit decisions can refine your judgment with knowledge.

Four Classes of Credit Information

What kinds of information are relevant to the evaluation of credit risk? An elaborate inquiry may not only be impossible but also unnecessary. Different business operations have different requirements. For example, a company which deals in low cost items and which does not expect its open accounts to reach large balances would not ask for the amount of credit information that the vendor of "big ticket" items would consider a bare minimum. An extended credit application in such a case would not only be unnecessary work, but it would also be resented by credit applicants.

One standard type of credit report groups the items of information it contains under four headings: Identity, history, character, and resources. This organization provides a good basis for discussion. It is felt that a complete credit application should provide some information in each of those areas.

1. *Identity*

Let us first look at the matter of identity. It is highly important to know to whom credit is being granted, and the name of the person is the most important item in establishing identity. It may seem strange to some that such a simple item should even require discussion. Simple and obvious it may be, but the name is crucial. It is not rare to find that John Smith, after getting into credit difficulties, becomes J. A. Smith and later, perhaps J. Alvin Smith. If necessary, other variations such as Jack Smith, Al Smith, or Jack A. Smith may be adopted. Persons of Latin extraction have a different tradition in the use of names which includes the family name of the female parent. In the process of anglicizing their names these individuals may innocently, or with intent, switch last names, anglicize first one part and then another, or confuse their identity in various other ways. It would seem that a minimum requirement on a credit application should be the *full* name. The full name, of course, would include such designators as "Jr.," "Sr.," and "III" when appropriate.

a. *Spelling of the Name.* Attention should also be given to the spelling of the name. Catharine Coffee may be quite a different person from Kathryn Cawfy. In fact, this one name may be spelled in 2,061 different ways. If there is any doubt about the matter, the spelling of the name should be resolved at the time the application is taken, not only for good credit practice, but also for good public relations. Improper spelling of a person's name can generate needless resentment. It is quite conceivable that some customer might deliberately delay payment because his name was spelled incorrectly on your statement. People are like that sometimes.

b. *Address.* Also included among the items which serve to establish identity is the address of the credit applicant and the length of his residence at that address. If the length of residence is short, the addresses of previous residences should be obtained. This inquiry encroaches on the material covered under history, and the length of time covered by the inquiry will vary with the type of credit being considered. Mortgage applications, for example, would usually go farther into the past than those for an open account with a department store.

c. *Age, Marital Status.* The age of the applicant should be obtained and, if there is any question about minority, the age should be verified. Marital status (single, married, divorced, widowed, or separated) should be included as well as the number and names of the other dependents. The name of the spouse should be included as well as his or her age and employment. If the applicant is a married man, one should not assume that his wife's occupation is only that of a housewife. About a third of the married women in the United States are also working, and knowledge about where a wife is employed can be useful if special collection effort becomes necessary

2. *History of employment*

One of the most important elements in the history is employment. The name and address of the present employer should be obtained. Also included should be length of employment, nature of position with the employer, and, if the period is brief, similar information on previous employment. If the present employer is a large firm, it is often convenient to have the badge or payroll number and the department in which the applicant works.

Special considerations for military personnel

Military personnel are a special problem. There are two major variables affecting the evaluation of military personnel as credit risks. The more important of these variables is, as could be expected, their rank or rating. Commissioned officers, who generally receive more generous incomes and who have been more carefully selected, are commonly considered to be good credit risks. As they advance in rank their incomes become larger and they are subjected to more and more rigorous screening. As a consequence, the higher the rank of the commissioned officer, the better is the significance of rank as an indicator of credit risk.

There is a considerable range of income among enlisted men. Those in the lowest pay grades must be considered poor credit risks on the basis of income alone. Those in the highest pay grades approach the point of financial equality with the lower ranks of commissioned officers. Their credit rating improves along with increased income.

Another variable to be considered when evaluating a serviceman is his reason for being in the service. The career serviceman is usually more concerned about his reputation in the service, both because of his desire for advancement and because the service is his community. He has cast his lot with the service, expects to stay with it, and wants to be well thought of by his associates. The draftee, on the other hand, may be less concerned about promotion and may also be strongly affected by his feelings concerning the temporary nature of his surroundings. He lacks roots in a permanent community where he feels known and about whose opinion he cares. As a consequence, the career serviceman is generally a better credit risk than the draftee.

Another problem in granting credit to military personnel arises out of the peculiar circumstances of their lives, especially their mobility. Military personnel are not only subject to unpredictable and sudden changes of station, but also sometimes do not themselves know in advance what their next more or less permanent address may be. Even the most conscientious person can forget a debt. If your statement cannot be delivered, the lapse of memory may become permanent.

Therefore, in granting credit to military personnel, it is most important to have a correct military address and correct service number. You should also get the permanent address, the home of parents or of the family. It is wise to obtain personal references, other than service personnel, as a start for tracing if this should become necessary.

3. *Character*

In order to evaluate character it is necessary to know how an individual has behaved in the past. An evaluation of this past performance may be obtained from credit references. You want the names of other companies with whom the applicant has, or has had, credit dealings, and the name of his bank, and the type or types of accounts he maintains, both at the bank and with his trade references. You would make inquiries of his trade references about his paying habits, noting if there are variations in his habits depending on the size or the type of account. You would look for evidence about his standard of living to see if it is in line with his income. For practical purposes, character is revealed in behavior. You want to know how he has behaved.

4. *Resources*

Many credit granters shy away from inquiring into resources. They often feel that the question, "What do you earn?", is offensive and improper. Yet most consumer credit is predicated more on future earnings than on present capital. Few charges to credit accounts will be paid out of currently owned resources. This is seldom the expectation either of the credit customer or the credit granter. The credit customer expects his income to continue at its present level, or to rise, and he typically plans to pay his charges out of future income. Since this is the case, a question about earnings would seem to be not only proper, but critical. When dealing with wage earners, it is the net pay about which you should be concerned. This is the sum from which payments must be made.

One oil company has found that, when a question about earnings is included in the application, 94 per cent of the applicants do answer. Perhaps inquiries about income are not as upsetting to the applicant as credit managers may feel. A statement about his income by the credit applicant is also valuable because most employers will verify or deny an employee's statement concerning income but will not give out income figures otherwise. It is definitely recommended that such a question be included on the credit application.

Since income is so important, a question about other sources of income should be included. This might be rents from real property, dividends from stock, or interest. Perhaps other members of the family are contributing. You also will be concerned about the stability of income. If the employer of the applicant is not well known, you may wish to inquire into the permanence of the employer.

Whether the applicant owns, rents, rooms, or boards is relevant to an evaluation of resources. If he rents, whether his quarters are furnished or unfurnished is pertinent information. Does he live in a trailer?

Does the applicant own an automobile? Is it financed? What is the balance due? How much are the payments? Does he have any other installment debt? Balance? Payments? Who could help him meet his obligation if he were disabled? The answers to all these questions are useful in making your evaluation.

The Application for Credit

Have applicant fill it out

In general, it seems preferable to have the applicant fill out the information himself. Although he may find the task somewhat of a chore, there is reason to believe that he is less hesitant about parting with personal information when he writes it himself than if he is responding aloud to questions posed by an interviewer.

Do not rely on interview

The interview should not necessarily be omitted, but it is only supplementary to the credit application. Insofar as the interview is an information-gathering process, its purpose is to clarify items on the application and to obtain the kind of information which cannot easily be asked by a direct question.

Have it signed

It is desirable, also, to have the application signed. There is a popular belief, particularly prevalent among persons from lower socio-economic levels, that no enforceable contract exists unless something has been signed. Asking for a signature gives an impression of legality to the process which also serves as an incentive to compliance with terms.

Requiring a signature also discourages some frauds. There is a reluctance to sign a name which is not one's own. Forgery is often felt to be a more serious transgression than cheating a business firm. The signature as a specimen of handwriting also may be of value as identifying information.

Ask for identification

Seldom, when taking an application, do credit granters ask for identification. Most persons carry identification with them and are quite willing to show it upon request. Such a procedure definitely lessens the chances of making mistakes in identification.

Give it a good name

Credit applicants are encouraged, sometimes, to be freer in responding to requests for information when the form they are asked to complete carries some title other than credit application. Consideration might be given to labeling it a service application or customer information blank. Names do make a difference. Consider the effect on sales if one of the popular brands of soap changed its name to Elmer's Animal Fat Soap. Certainly you would not advertise that a product was "cheap and flimsy"; rather you would call it "light and economical." The same principle can be used in credit practices.

Explain your terms

Later credit problems will be minimized if the terms are openly and courteously explained at the time the account is opened. Terms of payment should not be concealed in fine print or glossed over hurriedly. A considerable portion of the expense in a credit operation results from the necessity of prodding slow payers into action. This can be diminished, although not eliminated, by a discussion of how and when payments are to be made when the account is opened. This is one of the important things to be accomplished in the interview.

Importance of Credit Bureaus

Up to this point the discussion has implied that the credit granter is very much on his own in obtaining the credit information on which he must base his decisions. This is, of course, not the case. Many communities have credit bureaus from which members may obtain further assurance. These credit bureaus are only as good as their members make them. One of their basic functions is to accumulate information in their files so that members can quickly evaluate credit applications. Although this information comes from various sources, the information which is reported to them by their members is some of the most important. The credit bureau also investigates for members and adds the results to its files. These investigations can be relatively simple or quite detailed.

If your credit bureau is to do the best job for you, you must take the responsibility for getting enough information on your applicants to enable it to give you a report. It is most important that you supply the bureau with adequate identifying data. Particularly in large communities, the credit bureau may have a number of "Edward Wasnewski's" in its files. It needs complete identification in order to locate and report on your Edward Wasnewski. Definitely you should furnish the bureau with the full name, correctly spelled. Next in importance to the name is the address. If the applicant has been at his current address for less than three years, give the previous address as well. Other information, such as name of spouse, age, and employer may help the bureau to identify your applicant and to locate information in its files.

Further, in order to help the credit bureau build its files, you should supply the bureau with the information you obtain from applicants. You should report other open accounts listed by your applicants, any accounts you decline, and accounts which go too much past due. Your credit bureau manager will be eager to explain to you what information he needs. In the long run you can only benefit by actively cooperating. The more you and other credit granters give to your bureau, the more helpful will be the reports of the bureau to you.

Kinds of Credit Bureau Reports

Credit bureaus have various types of reports and conduct investigations of greater and lesser scope. Their charges depend on the elaborateness of the report or the investigation required. Your local bureau will be glad to supply you with a schedule of its services including both descriptions and charges.

Most bureaus make a distinction between telephone reports and written ones in their schedule of fees. Written ones, of course, cost more. Also, you can usually expect to pay more if you ask that your report be rushed or specify some particular deadline.

File check

The simplest type of report is offered by all bureaus under various names. It is sometimes called a file check and sometimes an in-file report. For most credit granters this type of report will take care of the majority of inquiries they will want to make. It consists merely of the bureau reading to the inquirer whatever information the bureau has in its file on the applicant. If the bureau does not have a record on that particular person, you will be told. If there is no record on file and the applicant's status indicates that there should be one, be alert. This is sometimes your clue to the fraud.

Negative report

Some bureaus make a distinction between the in-file report when information is given to you, and the negative report which states merely that there is no file. Care in providing the bureau with accurate identifying information will reduce the number of cases in which the search reveals no file.

Trade report

Another class of report is often called a trade report, although it, too, is known by other names. This report checks the trade references given by the applicant. The bureau will usually check the date the accounts were opened, the highest balances of the accounts, and the manner in which they were paid. Some bureaus will also check on accounts not listed by the applicant, but which their records show as places where the applicant has had credit. Some bureaus will obtain the amount currently owed on trade references checked by them.

Special report

You will be able to order a number of special reports on which you can obtain such things as verification of employment, age, marital status, number of dependents, home address, and employment. The bureau will investigate bank references. If the account is a checking account, it will seek the approximate average size of the balance. When the account is a savings account, the size of the account is not available without written permission from the credit applicant. The bureau will try to determine whether the applicant rents or owns his home, although it usually does not go through public records for this information. The credit bureau will also attempt to check on the character of the applicant through inquiries made of references.

If the credit granter has obtained adequate information of the kind suggested in this chapter, he is in a position to make fairly sound decisions about the credit risks he will take. By the use of information obtained through his own efforts, supplemented by that furnished through the credit bureau, if necessary, he should be able to decide with a fair degree of accuracy to what extent he is taking chances. He should also be in a position to recover the maximum amount from those few accounts which fail to pay on schedule.

Information about the individuals to whom you extend credit is essential for intelligent control of your risks. You should have all applicants supply you with enough information to enable you to estimate their credit worth, to enforce collection if it should become necessary, and to evaluate your own experience in making credit decisions. A good credit application will contain accurate and complete identification of the applicant, together with information about his personal history, his character, and his financial resources. Cooperation with your local credit bureau and judicious use of its facilities will add significantly to the amount and accuracy of your data.

INTERVIEWING CREDIT APPLICANTS

III

INTERVIEWING CREDIT APPLICANTS

The credit interview is a conversation with three major purposes. The first and most obvious of these purposes is to secure information. The second purpose is to instruct future customers in credit terms and policies. Last, but by no means least, it should be your purpose to influence the future customers in such a way that they will be well disposed toward your company; in short, to make them like you.

Securing Information

You are most apt to secure accurate and complete information from the applicant if you approach him with forthright honesty and frankness. The interviewer should not attempt to be shrewd, subtle, or try to out-guess the applicant. Cleverness in interviewing is out of place. Your attitude should, rather, be one of cooperation. Both the interviewer and the applicant are working together toward a mutual goal, opening an account. Your applicant will be frank if he feels that you will not take unfair advantage of what is said. He will give you information if he feels (1) you have a right to the information, (2) that your questions are relevant, and (3) the end is to his advantage.

Tell the applicant your purpose

The applicant should understand the purpose of the interview, and he should accept that purpose as his own. To this end you should state the reasons for the interview clearly and in language he can understand. Quite sincerely tell him that the information is needed in order to enable you to open the account and to make available to him the services he wants.

Put him at ease

Your first step is to put the applicant at ease. Rise to meet him. Call him by name, perhaps engage in a few pleasantries, and wait until the initial nervousness has passed. Indicate by your manner that you are glad to have him present. Be interested, sincere, and natural. Treat him much as if he were a guest in your own home.

Pre-plan the interview

It is best if you have examined the application before you see the applicant. You are then able to plan your interview and to decide what you want to accomplish. Further, scanning the application while the applicant is present may be perceived as rude or threatening. Check for blank spaces or incomplete answers on the application. Make note of these things so that you will not miss clearing them up during the interview.

Make it natural

You should also have an interview guide which has headings for the general areas into which you wish to inquire. Although this guide should have a few illustrative questions, they should not be fired at the applicant in an inquisitorial manner. Let the conversation develop naturally, but steer it into the areas on which you want information. Display an interest in what the applicant is saying and interject your questions where they are appropriate. Learn to listen actively, not absently.

Keep it private

By all means, arrange to have the interview in a place that is private and free from interfering noises or distractions. Your credit applicant will appreciate the courtesy and will be much more inclined to discuss confidential matters in such a setting.

Put yourself in his place

While you are interviewing the applicant, try putting yourself in his place. Use your imagination. What would you think and feel if you were in his spot?

Watch your time

Do not rush the interview. Allow plenty of time. The customer likes to feel that he is the most important matter you have to attend to at the moment. Moreover, if the atmosphere is unhurried, the applicant is more likely to volunteer valuable information which would not be elicited by direct questions.

On the other hand, do not waste time. The objective of the interview is not just to have a pleasant chat. You have a purpose and you should accomplish it without undue delay. Remember, you may be wasting the applicant's time, too, and this could be resented.

Keep on the subject

Do not allow the interview to wander off the topic. Be tactful in bringing the conversation back to the matter at hand. Do not just allow the conversation to drift. Time for the interview is not limitless.

Save touchy topics for last

Begin your interview with matters which are least likely to encounter resistance and leave the more sensitive areas until later in the conversation. When the situation has warmed up and the applicant feels easier, more intimate questions may be discussed.

Understand and be understood

Be careful to make your questions clear and distinct, both with respect to your language and your articulation. You can get wrong answers simply because your questions were misunderstood by the applicant. Watch your wording and avoid ambiguity in your questions.

If you are not quite sure you understood an answer correctly, clear the matter up. One way to do this is to repeat the answer you thought you heard and ask if it is correct. Above all, do not guess; know what was said.

Phrase questions carefully

In your questioning, do not phrase your questions so that they suggest an answer. Such questions as, "You don't have accounts at any other stores?" "No balance is outstanding, is it?" or "It is an installment account you are opening, isn't it?" very clearly point the way to certain answers. The same information can be better sought by the positive forms, "At what stores do you have accounts?" "What is the balance?" and "What kind of an account do you wish to open?"

Make notes

Record the information you obtain during the interview. Do not wait until the applicant has left. Memory is a tricky thing and can distort facts.

Be open-minded

Do not pre-judge the applicant. Keep an open mind and avoid letting your own prejudices or biases influence your attitude or your judgment.

All of these cautions will help you to achieve each of the three purposes of the interview. They are, however, mainly designed to help you to achieve the first objective—obtaining information. It should be emphasized that this is, by all means, the least important of the three. If the credit interview had no purpose other than to obtain credit information, it could be dispensed with and the credit granter would scarcely feel the lack.

Oil companies, national credit card companies, and mail order houses grant credit on the basis of written information alone. Many other businesses do the same thing even though the necessity for dispensing with the interview does not exist. Their credit losses are not appreciably greater as a result of this policy. Perhaps the written application with no personal interview at all is not the best procedure for evaluating credit risk, but the fact that it succeeds at all indicates that the supplementary information developed during the interview cannot, in itself, justify the added expense and time involved.

The only justification for the time and expense involved in personal interviews with credit applicants must be found in the other two purposes: teaching customers about credit terms and motivating them to use the account they are opening. Unless these purposes are served, the credit interview is a needless additional expense, surviving in retail stores through the force of custom and usage only. Whoever does the interviewing should be thoroughly aware of this point. Although the credit interview may purport to be a means of getting information, this is actually a subsidiary purpose.

Make Known Credit Terms and Policies

At some time during the credit interview, credit terms should be explained. The customer should become aware of your need for prompt payment and understand the reasonableness of this policy. Perhaps some mention of the costs involved in bookkeeping and collection can be brought into the conversation. In this way you may indicate that, through a firm arrangement for promptness, your prices can be kept lower. If it is an installment account which is being opened, you should quite specifically state when the next payment is due and the amount of that payment. It is not necessary to make a big issue of the matter at any particular juncture, but you should seek opportunities as they arise during the conversation.

Selling Your Company

Selling your company is one of the most critical functions. Cordiality, a warm smile, and a cheerful greeting are indispensable. Courteous attention to everything the applicant says, an attitude of service, and a sensitivity to the applicant's feelings will help to establish the kind of relations which will make the applicant want to do business with you. Do not fail to accord the gilt-edged credit risk the deference he feels is his due. If the application shows clearly that this customer is unquestionably sound, do not feel that it is necessary to probe and pry, or even to prolong the interview. Use the time you have to flatter this customer and conclude, as in all interviews, with some sincere and natural remark such as, "It has been a pleasure to serve you."

You will be most effective both in selling your company and in getting information if your attitude is sincere and open. You should pre-plan your interview and arrange for it to take place in a private and relaxed atmosphere. Neither rush nor prolong the matter. Stay on the subject and reserve sensitive areas for the last. Be sure you and the applicant understand one another and record information immediately. At this point you *are* the company to the applicant. Make him want to do business with *you.*

Of the three purposes for conducting a credit interview, the most important is a sales function. Of secondary importance is educating the customers to prompt payment in accordance with terms. The least important of all is the ostensible purpose of obtaining information. Credit information may be obtained more cheaply, more reliably, and more quickly than through personal interview.

EVALUATING CREDIT RISK

IV

EVALUATING CREDIT RISK

Credit information is obtained only to be used. First, it is used to provide the data for a decision. One must decide, on the basis of the information available, whether or not to extend credit to this individual and, sometimes, to assign a dollar limit to that credit. In most consumer credit situations, this decision is made as a result of the subjective weighing of the evidence. It is based on the judgment of credit personnel with more or less experience in such matters. The accuracy of these judgments depends both on the knowledge these persons have concerning the significance of the information provided and upon their own temperaments. Some things can be said about both knowledge and temperament.

The Three "C's" of Credit—Character, Capacity, and Capital

The traditional three "C's" of credit—character, capacity, and capital—still provide a good basis for evaluating credit risk. Character refers to the behavior of an individual, how he has handled his obligations and responsibilities. Specifically, you want to know whether or not you can rely upon him to honor his commitments. Capacity and capital deal with his resources for implementing his good intentions. You want to know if he has the *capacity* for producing the funds necessary to handle his obligations and, if need arise, whether his present *capital* is enough to liquidate his debts. These three "C's" are not independent of one another. Usually capital is the result of past capacity and is, therefore, some evidence of capacity for future production. Likewise, capacity for producing income commonly hinges on character. The unreliable individual is less likely to earn a position commanding a high income. Thus, the three "C's" are correlated. Those individuals who have high ratings in any one tend also to have high ratings in the others. Nevertheless, it is possible to view each item of credit information as contributing mainly to evaluation of one or another of these three "C's."

What's his name?

Let us first look at the significance of some of the information we presumably have on the credit applicant. The name of the applicant is of little significance in the evaluation of credit risk. There are those who attach importance to the national origin suggested by the name. These persons feel that they obtain clues about the cultural background of an individual from the nationality of his name. They believe in the stereotype of the "thrifty Germans," "the fiery French," or the "honest Danes." Some contend that one can draw a line across a map of Europe and separate the good risk nationalities in the north from the poorer risk nationalities in the south. Although there are differences in the values attached to various kinds of behavior among, say, Latin, Germanic, and Scandinavian peoples, the evidence provided by the name about the possession of these attitudes by any individual is so slight as to deserve little attention. The differences among the individuals within a nationality group are greater than the differences among the nationalities themselves.

Where does he live?

The address of the applicant is a critical matter; it may provide quite important signals and clues about character. Certain areas tend to be high risk areas while others are low risk areas. Delinquent debtors tend to cluster in certain neighborhoods within a community. For example, in Chicago, a city with over 200 square miles of expanse, the Collection Division of the Credit Bureau of Cook County found, in a sampling of its accounts, that six per cent of the accounts referred to it for collection were on persons living within a single square mile. There were other areas which were also high risk areas. In general these were economically depressed neighborhoods which also tended to be areas in which juvenile delinquency rates were high and other forms of social disorganization were present.

Certainly not all credit problems are associated with such circumstances; they are met in all neighborhoods at all economic levels. However, no student of sociology would be surprised to find that problem debtors are concentrated in areas characterized by anonymity and a general lack of social control.

Because such areas do exist, you should be familiar with your community so that you know the character of the neighborhood from an address. You should know which are residential areas, which are primarily industrial and commercial areas, where rooming houses are common, which are apartment areas, and where trailer courts are found. You will specifically note such questionable addresses as those of rooming houses, hotels and trailer courts. Applicants from high risk areas would receive more careful scrutiny.

In addition to the character of the neighborhood in which an applicant lives, attention should be given to his length of residence. Stability, and its usual companion, responsibility, are ordinarily accompanied by a degree of geographical permanence. Unless frequent changes of address can be justified by the nature of an individual's occupation, they should be viewed with suspicion. Although the people of the United States are becoming geographically more mobile (about 20 per cent change address every year), moves which are too frequent may point to a restlessness which can result in financial difficulties. Ordinarily, ownership of a home and furnishings is a positive sign indicating both stability and the possession of some assets. If the size of the mortgage is known, it should be considered. Some people over-extend themselves to put on a front.

Home ownership has, in recent years, lost some of its significance as a result of trends in the home building industry. Some newer homes are of less durable construction and, in some cases, there is even cause to wonder if the building will outlast the mortgage. This circumstance, when coupled with questionable plans for financing the purchase of the dwelling, makes it difficult or impossible for the supposed "owner" actually to obtain a real or realizable equity. Credit men should be aware of such housing developments and adjust their evaluations accordingly.

How does he make his living?

Frequent changes of occupation are an unfavorable sign. The job-jumper often is unstable both in temperament and income. Changes of employment are less significant among younger individuals who frequently do a little floundering before they reach an occupational adjustment. Among older and, supposedly, more mature persons, such behavior becomes a more pernicious sign. In order to judge the occupational stability of an applicant, you can probably assume that an individual who has been with one employer for three years or more is fairly well settled in his occupation.

Occupational stability should be evaluated in relation to the effect which the moves have had on the occupational level of the applicant. They have somewhat less significance if it appears that the applicant has consistently bettered his position by moving. They are more unfavorable if the moves have been lateral, and they are most unfavorable if they are associated with a drop in his earning power. A similar factor should be considered with respect to changes of residence. A rapidly rising young man may find it necessary to change his address often as he climbs.

The occupation of the applicant is, of course, important in determining credit risk. In general, the higher the occupation is in social status or prestige, the better is the indication of good credit risk. Persons with prestige and status have usually earned their positions through a history of responsible behavior. They can be expected to continue to behave responsibly in the future. Further, such persons value their positions and are hesitant to do anything which might injure their standing. Lastly, people tend to behave much in the ways others expect of them, and the public demands responsible behavior of some while it is not so exacting of others. For example, a truck driver can have a noisy good time in a local tavern without causing eyebrows to rise. If, however, a well-known physician did the same, many people would be scandalized. The physician would suffer a loss of status and, perhaps, of income as well. It is a matter of conforming to what is considered right for one's role in the community.

Certain classes of occupations are usually good credit risks, while others are, generally speaking, not as good. Professional persons (physicians, dentists, engineers, etc.), management personnel, skilled workers (tool and die makers, machinists, millwrights, etc.), and white collar workers are among the better risks. Some occupations which are widely considered hazardous from a credit viewpoint are these: bartender, cook, waitress, bell boy, entertainer, night club operator, cab driver, trucker, and general laborer.

Self-employed persons form a separate category. If they are the owners of established businesses in reputable fields, they are usually good risks personally. If their business is done in questionable areas, their integrity may be suspect. In other words, an evaluation of the credit worth of a self-employed person should hinge on an evaluation of his business. You should look at profitability, respectability, and the length of time he has been in business. Self-employed individuals (and we must include lawyers in this group) are among the most difficult persons to collect from when their accounts "go sour."

What does he earn?

In evaluating the significance of the employment information, regularity of earnings should be considered. Seasonal employment or earnings may be considered as a possible adverse sign. It takes better than average foresight and maturity to plan and to budget for a fluctuating income. There is a tendency to live well while the money is coming in and to tighten belts when times are not so good. When the belt is tightened, past obligations are more likely to be postponed than are current wants. Some persons even feel that they have a moral right to a moratorium on their debts when they meet with such reverses. Their thinking may go something like this, "My business was good enough for them when I had it rolling in, but, now that I've had a little bad luck, they're pushing me for a few measly bucks." Capacity refers to *future* income, and *present* earnings are only an indication of this. What the applicant is making now is less important than what he will make in the next two, six, or twelve months.

Is he married? children?

Some of the indications to be gleaned from marital status are rather obvious. Married persons are usually better credit risks than are single ones. Many credit men believe that single women are better risks than single men. Those who are divorced or separated are usually the greatest hazards during the first year after divorce or separation. If you have reason to know of marital strife, the possibility of divorce or separation poses important credit problems and may turn an otherwise good bet into a bad debt.

Marital status, as such, is significant mainly as a clue to character. It tells you something about the applicant's willingness to assume responsibility—not necessarily how he handles the responsibility. The presence of children in the family increases his moral responsibilities but not in proportion to the number of children. Three children constitute little more of a moral responsibility than do two. The number of dependents is more important as it relates to capacity. How well does the applicant's income permit him to provide for a family of his size?

If the number of dependents is not out of line with income, a married man with a family is better from a credit point of view than a married man without children. You should be cautious if the applicant has more than three children, while six or more children form a heavy financial burden for anyone who is not in a top income bracket. Unless there is evidence to indicate a capacity to produce income to match family productivity, the application should be viewed with disfavor.

How old is he?

Age is an important factor. Partly because of legal issues, most credit granters do not extend credit to minors. Those who do, usually require that the account be guaranteed by a responsible adult. There are some few companies, however, who have been tempted by the teen-age market and are experimenting with credit granting to this group without guaranty. It would not be surprising to see this trend broaden.

Even if the applicant is of legal age, those who are under 25 seem to be poorer risks than those who are older. When evaluating younger males, you should consider their status with respect to military service. If they are likely to be drafted, this fact constitutes a hazard to their incomes and to any creditors they may owe. The anonymity of military service, the lack of roots, and the frequent changes of address may undermine the good intentions of a young man who would have been a perfectly sound risk had he stayed at home. In considering age in this way, we are primarily concerned with character.

In some circumstances, particularly in long-term installment credit, advanced age also may be viewed as a minus factor. Most men reach their peak years both of income and consumption during their forties. On the average both income and consumption fall during subsequent decades. With advancing age, too, a declining percentage is employed. More are living on fixed dollar incomes, which means, in times of inflation, a shrinking purchasing power. Too, there is the increasing mortality rate to be considered. When considering credit for older persons, you should give greater attention to the matter of capital than you would with younger individuals. Age, viewed in this light, bears on capacity and capital.

The significance of age as a credit fact must be interpreted in relation to other factors. Some persons became socially and emotionally mature at a much earlier chronological age than do others. Some never become mature in this sense. Other evidences of stability and responsibility culled from the occupational and personal history must be considered. What you should be looking for is maturity, not just age. Maturity, of course, is a matter of character.

Consider the contrast in these two cases. Both members of the first couple are 24 years of age. The husband is an assembler in a factory. They have four children. Nevertheless, they have acquired a substantial equity in a home; they add occasionally to their small savings account; and they owe installments only on one item at a time. The members of the second couple are exactly the same age and have two children. The husband has held a variety of jobs, but none long enough to become established. His longest period of steady employment has been ten months. In spite of this, he has been able to obtain enough credit that he has already voluntarily taken bankruptcy.

One wonders what basis the creditors of the second young man found for extending credit. His behavior certainly did not show either social or economic maturity in any sense.

There are other implications of age. If the wife is 25 or less she may be entering the period of bearing and rearing a family. As a result one should not count heavily on any contribution she is making to the family income. In fact, the possibility of increased demands on the husband's salary should be kept in mind. If the wife is over 35, more reliance may be placed on her earnings as an indicator of capacity.

Age, then, is a fact which must be considered in the evaluation of all of the three "C's." It bears on character (maturity, responsibility, and stability), capacity (an estimation of future earning power and the demands which will be made upon it), and capital (the adequacy of the estate to handle obligations). The implications of age should be examined from each viewpoint.

What is his record?

Last, and most important, are the facts about the applicant's past behavior which can be obtained from checking trade references, banking references, and with credit bureaus. Has this person demonstrated his willingness and ability to use his credit properly and to pay his obligations promptly? This is a critical question. If the answer to it is "yes," that fact scores a convincing plus. If the answer is "no," you should proceed with extreme caution.

The farther you can go into past time and still document responsible financial behavior, the stronger this indicator becomes. Some persons under 25 who have been divorced less than a year, living in a rooming house in a high risk area, and who are working as laborers in a road gang, will yet pay every dollar they owe exactly on the date due. Such a man is a better credit risk than the homeowner of 40 with two children, who lives in a fancy suburb, but who shows a history of judgments and collection accounts. A casual comparison of these two individuals on routine criteria would give wrong results. It is only when past behavior is examined that we see the difference that makes a difference, a history of responsible behavior versus a history of irresponsible behavior.

Attitudes toward credit obligations are part of the sense of right and wrong, and these attitudes are inculcated early in the life history of an individual. They are deeply ingrained and changed slowly. The best possible predictor of an individual's future behavior is his past performance.

There are anecdotes and tall tales which may appear to refute this principle, but, even if true, they are isolated instances and no predictor of human behavior is without exceptions. One hears about the wastrel who found the right woman and has since been a model of virtue, or the criminal who awoke one morning and, seeing the error of his ways, sinned no more. Such things may happen, but a smart gambler would not bet on them. The credit granter should not do so either.

The credit man who bases his decisions on appearance, manner, speech, poise, the "ring of sincerity," or favorite interviewing questions or stunts is destined to err more often than is necessary. He will be money ahead if he makes his decisions on a dispassionate appraisal of facts and dismisses the applicant's personal impact as much as possible.

Despite errors which should have been convincing and despite mountains of experimental evidence to the contrary, those who believe they can judge a man's character in a brief interview doggedly cling to this illusion. That such persons continue to exist in the credit business is not so much a tribute to their insight as it is to the fact that they are playing with loaded dice.

The truth is that most people pay their bills. The approval of a credit application, even without evaluating it, has a better chance of being right than of being wrong. The entire process of evaluating credit risk is merely an attempt to eliminate some of the already small percentage of bad risks without excluding too many of the potentially good ones. The gullible credit man is playing with the odds, but his mistakes eventually become known. The suspicious credit man is playing against the odds, but his mistakes seldom come to light. The temperament of the credit man is probably an essential determinant of the direction a company leans in its credit risk taking.

Temperament—Do you have a bias?

In recent years psychologists have become aware of a phenomenon which may have important implications in the selection of credit men. In the building of tests, psychologists often formulate questions so that they can be answered *yes* or *no* and *agree* or *disagree.* It has been discovered that some persons have a disposition to answer *yes,* or to agree, which is so strong that it outweighs the content of the question itself. Other persons have a similar but opposite tendency to say *no* or to disagree, regardless of the question posed. Further, and more important for credit granters, this tendency appears to go beyond psychological test behavior and to reflect a basic facet of personality. Those who are agreers or "yes-men" tend to be more extroverted socially, to speak easily about themselves, and to react more obviously to their own moods. The disagreers or "no-men" are more introverted, tend to lack social spontaneity, and to answer questions more indirectly. The "yes-men" are more impulsive and crave excitement, while the "no-men" are more controlled and try harder to be rational and sensible. The important point is that this bias to say "no" in situations stems from a temperamental characteristic which is consistent over long periods of time and which generalizes to other life situations. It is quite possible that many credit men are, by temperament, "no-men" and that others are temperamentally "yes-men." Individual bias could conceivably be more important than credit policy.

Weighted application—Fool-proof formula?

In some credit-granting situations, the influence of temperament and judgment is minimized by the use of standard criteria such as weighted credit applications. When such a method is used, a certain number of points is assigned for each positive indication in the credit application and, perhaps, subtracted for each negative item. The sum of these points must equal some established total before an account is considered acceptable. Some of these credit "score cards," as such devices are sometimes called, have been evolved merely on the opinions of experienced credit men as to the importance of each indicator and an arbitrary weighting has been assigned to each on the basis of these opinions. Some large credit granters, such as mail order houses, have been able to accumulate sufficient data on their credit experience to apply statistical research techniques and arrive at weightings based on mathematical analysis.

One technique for arriving at such devices studies the relationships among all the items of credit information given and tries to develop weights for each item which, when added, will yield a score which ranks credit applicants in order. This means that an applicant whose credit score card gives a total of 50 is presumably a better risk than one who gets 45 even though both may be acceptable. This continuous gradation of credit risk is handy if one wishes to be able to change the risk level from time to time as conditions change. Under one set of circumstances the company may wish to be selective. At such a time the acceptable score is merely raised. When it is desired to liberalize credit granting the acceptable criterion score is lowered.

Another technique which may be used to arrive at weightings for a credit score card is designed to arrange matters so that the differences in the scores of good credit risks and bad credit risks are maximized. It is not so much interested in ranking the risks in order as it is in making sure that the bad credit risk has a low enough score to stand out. This method is of greatest use where large risks are possible, where credit is being granted in substantial amounts. It protects more against a loss of capital than against a loss of potential profits.

Such mathematical weighting techniques depend on the amassing of accurate research information concerning credit experience. Good and complete credit applications, together with the subsequent behavior of the applicants, must be available. The mathematical techniques will then tell what combination of weights would have produced results in the past. The assumption is that your future applicants will be similar to those of past and that the same indicators will predict their behavior. This assumption is not always justified, particularly when a change in policy produces a different clientele.

The credit granter often lacks the high-level mathematical training necessary to develop such applications, but the services of mathematicians and statisticians can be obtained on a consultant basis. Those who decide to use such methods should be certain that they understand the logic involved in their development even if the methods by which they are developed remain a mystery. Lacking such an understanding, one might well demand or expect too much of the results.

Weighted credit applications would seem to be most useful in situations where large numbers of credit decisions must be made by relatively untrained clerks. They would be less useful when the number of credit applications to be processed is small and the individual responsible for their evaluation is able to exercise judgment. Weighted applications have the advantages of mechanizing the credit-granting process and of minimizing the cost of screening, but they also tend to reject the marginal risk who might have been a profitable customer and who might have been accepted by an experienced credit man. Weighted credit applications can only include what they were built to include. They will not consider exceptional circumstances.

Combining the weighted credit application with judgment eliminates some of these faults of the system but also some of the advantages. The purpose of using weighted applications is to reduce the amount of individual decision needed. Adding, again, the factor of judgment, partially defeats this goal. Rejecting all credit applicants below a stated score, accepting all above a certain level, and requiring judgments to be made by higher-level personnel on those who fall in a twilight zone between the two criteria scores may be an acceptable compromise in some situations.

The use of weighted applications can help the beginning credit man screen out bad risks and pass the obviously good ones. He can then refer the marginal or questionable risks to a more experienced person for final decision. This not only frees the experienced credit man from the routine of clear-cut cases but also provides an excellent opportunity for training the novice in the subtleties of credit decisions. Do not leave decisions in the "muddy" or questionable area to clerks relying on a formula.

Two Approaches to Estimating Risk

There is nothing particularly abstruse or mysterious about the evaluation of credit risk. Essentially, it is an effort to predict future behavior from present information. One cannot, of course, know in advance how any given individual will behave in the future. Any prediction is merely a guess and the best that can be expected is to do somewhat better than chance alone would do.

In predicting human behavior there are two basic approaches. The first approach is to examine the present and past behavior of the individual in question and then to predict that his future behavior will be similar to his past behavior. The credit granter uses this approach when he checks trade references and considers character. The assumption is that individuals show a degree of consistency, that they seldom change drastically in their fundamental natures.

The other approach is to compare the individual in question with other persons who are similar to him in certain relevant characteristics. One then predicts that the future behavior of that individual will be like that which has been observed in the similar persons. The credit man does this when he considers address, occupation or marital status. Here the assumption is that, since the applicant is like others in these respects, he will be like them in his paying habits.

Neither method is completely accurate. Human behavior is not completely predictable by any means now known. One is forced to rely on general principles and a knowledge of certain danger signals.

Some of the danger signals of credit have been summarized by the Credit Bureau of Greater New York. They are important for every credit granter.

PERSONAL DANGER SIGNALS

1. Residence in: rooming house; hotel; in care of a friend; furnished apartment; slovenly home or section; place where questionable people are known to reside.
2. People in modest financial circumstances, with large dependent family.
3. Individuals on whom it is impossible to obtain prior history and on whom authorities at the residence and business locations did not check on arrival or employment.
4. People who open several new accounts on a moderate or small income.
5. Persons suspected of being irresponsible minors; alcoholics; mentally unstable; drug addicts.
6. Single persons living away from home on whom background information is not available.
7. Women who live under desirable conditions, who refuse or have failed to furnish sources of income or reliable references.
8. Divorced or separated women or widows who cannot supply financial references.
9. People who are in an extreme hurry to obtain credit at a time when it is difficult or impossible to obtain credit information.
10. Individuals who try to impress the credit granter with their extreme desirability as credit risks.
11. People under foreign rule or special laws, such as: nationals of other countries on visitors' permits, without U. S. funds; applicants from blocked-currency nations, and Indians living on reservations.
12. People who claim good incomes which cannot be verified, who do not carry a regular checking account.

OCCUPATIONAL DANGER SIGNALS

13. Employment with a small, unknown firm, or with a relative.
14. Generally unstable or hazardous occupation, such as bartender; dishwasher; taxi driver; longshoreman; day laborer; counterman; laundry worker; nurse; maid; waiter housekeeper; garage worker.
15. Individuals who work in glamorous but relatively poor-paying jobs, such as chorus girls or boys, models, dance hall hostesses.
16. Business people who rent desk space or telephone service only, and cannot furnish good bank or business references.

17. People who work for employers who are known as questionable or unreliable.
18. People who work for organizations so small that they may be answering the telephone themselves when an employment verification is sought.
19. People who make a living on fees earned at home, such as music teachers, tutors, masseurs, fortune tellers.
20. Salesmen who work for out-of-town concerns, whose length of service, earnings and reliability cannot readily be established.
21. Salesmen who work on a commission basis only.
22. Individuals "in business for themselves at the home address," who cannot furnish bank references and evidence of the scope of their business, such as names of suppliers and/or customers.
23. Transient employees such as nurses; demonstrators; campaign fund workers; solicitors.
24. People who work for businesses which are as a class unreliable or subject to racketeering such as vending machine companies, horse racing, "dope" sheets, carnival workers.
25. People who claim to be "retired," but on whom past history and bank or financial references or evidence of wealth cannot be established.
26. Purchases made on accounts carried in firm or corporate names, for personal use of individuals.*

Although changing economic condtions may alter the significance of specific signals, the basic problem of prediction does not change. The evaluation of credit risk is an attempt to see into the future and to forecast how persons will behave with respect to the trust placed in them. These predictions will continue to be made on the basis of comparisons with similar individuals and the past performance of the individuals themselves.

* E. M. Arthur, *Checking and Rating the New Account* (New York: Credit Management Division, National Retail Merchants Association, 1960), pp. 43–45.

ROUTINE COLLECTIONS

V

ROUTINE COLLECTIONS

As stated earlier, most people pay their bills. The exact figures for different periods of delinquency vary according to the character of the risks which are taken, the kind of goods or services sold, the nature of the contract, the credit-granting procedures, billing practices, and the general health of the economy. Most credit granters find that over three-fourths of their accounts are paid on time, and that only a very small percentage allows them to go 90 days. Many obtain even higher percentages of prompt payment. We tend to take this high degree of conformity for granted just as we take for granted the fact that most people we encounter speak English. Our attention is caught by the exceptions, those who do not exhibit the expected pattern of behavior. We seek explanations for the unusual but, because the usual is commonplace, we accept it uncritically. Sometimes, however, an examination of the rule can explain the exception.

Habits and Paying Bills

This remarkable degree of conformity in bill-paying behavior is certainly not the result of any built-in biological urge to part with money on the tenth of the month or even at any specific part of the lunar cycle. Indeed the kind of complex pattern of credit purchasing and repayment which is so predictable in our particular society is not even seen in other lands and times.

The use of credit is not peculiar to our culture. In one form or another, credit is world wide, and its use antedates written history. Conceivably the first credit transaction involved an exchange of dinosaur steaks or stone axes. However, our forms of consumer credit, the 30-day charge, the installment plan, revolving credit, etc., are largely products of the twentieth century as are the usages and practices surrounding these forms. Our billing practices, methods of obtaining credit, ways of exchanging credit information, and collection techniques are of fairly modern origin.

The high degree of conformity in repayment of debts cannot be satisfactorily explained as the result of a general trait of honesty. We can observe that one individual is scrupulously honest about paying his bills even though he is embezzling the money to do so from his employer. A man may be punctilious about honesty at cards and nevertheless lie to his wife, cheat on his income tax, and shamelessly misrepresent his product in his advertising. A thief may see no contradiction between stealing in one situation and not stealing in another.

Do People Pay Because They Are Honest?

A number of psychological studies indicate that honesty is not a general trait of behavior but is, instead, specific to a situation. Moreover, an explanation of credit behavior in terms of honesty begs the question. We say a man is honest because he pays his bills and then we explain his bill-paying behavior by saying he is honest. This is an explanation which does not explain; it merely describes. One must look elsewhere for an explanation of the fact that such a large proportion of the population pays its bills and pays them on time. This explanation may be found in the typical life history of a human being in a society.

Growing Up and Paying Bills

When born, the human infant understands and perceives little or nothing. He has to learn the meaning of the sights, sounds, and smells which surround him. As he grows older he begins to identify some of these sights and sounds as other people, and he begins to learn that these people have rather definite ideas about how he should behave. He discovers that if he does certain things they will scold and punish, while if he does others they will smile and praise. The attitudes of these other people vitally affect his satisfactions and his comfort. He learns to do those things which bring him satisfactions and to avoid those which bring pain.

From infancy on, the human being is dependent on others for the satisfaction of his physical and psychological needs. His existence does not depend so much on his individual skills in obtaining nourishment from nature or in protecting himself from natural forces as it does on his ability to make the complex patterns of sounds we call speech. The welfare of a human being in society hinges primarily on his skills in obtaining the approval and cooperation of other human beings.

Sociologists and social psychologists explain the development of moral behavior, of which honoring one's promises is a part, in terms of this process of socialization. In the course of living with other members of various groups, the individual learns the rituals, laws, taboos, rules, and standard practices which these groups consider right and proper for him to follow. He picks up the habits, attitudes, and values of people in the groups he feels at home with, to which he feels he belongs.

The first such group in the lives of most persons is the family, and a very significant part of moral behavior is learned in this first group. The child learns his standards of moral behavior from experiencing the consequences of "right" and "wrong" behavior, from imitating the behavior of other family members, and from verbal precepts. In one family, the child who pockets a candy bar at the grocery may be marched back in shame and forced tearfully to confess his crime. In another family, the child may be scolded but allowed to keep his loot, while in yet another, he may meet with tacit or even open approval. In one family the child may hear his father openly boast of his success in cheating or "conning" someone else. In another, the father may be loud in his protestations of the virtues of honesty and yet brag of evading a portion of his income taxes. All of these experiences are absorbed by the child with the result that he learns not only what moral principles he should follow, but also which ones he should only profess.

Some Human Behavior Is Predictable

Later, the individual becomes a member of other groups: a school, a gang, a clique, a work group, a church, a club, and a number of others. In all of these associations he reacts to the pressures of others to adopt certain kinds of behaviors and to avoid other kinds. He continues learning, to a greater or lesser degree, to do what is expected of him. This socialization process produces the typical behavior one has learned to expect of others, e.g., that American men wear pants rather than kilts, that when you smile and offer your hand the other will take it, and that "Thank you" will be answered by "You're welcome," or words to that effect. You bet your life each day on your ability to predict this kind of conforming behavior. You cross the street confidently when the light is green, expecting cross traffic to stop. You drive without fear on the right side of the road, scarcely considering the possibility that another car proceeding in the opposite direction might be met on your side. There is nothing inherently "natural" about any of this behavior. It was all tediously and slowly taught to each individual by the process of socialization.

Why People Do Not Pay

If we understand bill-paying behavior in these terms we can see many different reasons for a non-conforming behavior of failing to pay. In the first place, the problem individual may have been an excellent product of his socialization. He may actually have learned to behave in the ways that were right and proper in the groups of which he was and is a member. Let us see how this could happen.

From his family the child may have received approval for contributing small items which he pilfered. His parents may have been amused to hear how he outwitted the "cop." He may have belonged to a gang in which he gained status by successfully defying the law. Cheating and deceiving persons outside the gang may have been the "smart" thing to do. True frauds and criminals are produced in this way by the same processes which lead to law-abiding behavior in others.

The background may not have been so extreme. The child may not have learned to be aggressively predatory, and yet have learned that rich people, large companies, and government agencies are proper victims for any cheating one can get away with. Evasion of debt could be considered a clever way to enrich one's self at the expense of those who "don't really need it."

Poor risk areas

Credit men are quite aware that certain families have more than their share of bad risks. Some neighborhoods are high risk areas. The transmission of the ethical standards of the group to its new members explains these phenomena.

Emotional problems

Although the usual standards may have been learned in the process of socialization, these lessons may sometimes be contrary to strong personal needs and motives. In this case, the individual may find himself in conflict between his moral training and his individual wants. If these wants stem from powerful drives, the individual may forget his training and obey his impulses. When this happens, his behavior appears to be "irrational," which is to say it does not follow the socialized pattern we expect. This can happen when a person is terrified, in the grip of a violent rage, or in the throes of a passionate love affair. Such a circumstance can be suspected when a person with a history of responsible behavior seems suddenly to become irresponsible. He may have been panicked by severe business reverses, infuriated by the treatment he received from the creditor's employee, or he may simply be infatuated. Credit problems arising from this cause may be puzzling but they are neither frequent nor difficult to resolve.

Failure to learn

Last, the socialized patterns, for some reason, may not have been learned. The individual has been exposed to the proper influences but the expected learning did not take place. This is a more important cause of credit problems.

The failure to learn can be the result of intellectual limitations. Some individuals lack the intellectual equipment to master all of the lessons society tries to teach its members. They simply cannot understand finance charges and interest. The terms of an installment contract are confusing to them. The budgeting of their funds is an impossibly complex operation. These persons are often the victims of unscrupulous individuals, but may also be the unintentional victims of others who fail to recognize their limitations. These intellectually limited persons find it difficult to manage their finances without the added complication of credit, and quite innocently become credit problems because they have not been able to learn what they need to know.

Some individuals appear to be emotionally incapable of accepting the responsibilities of adult life. They seem to be more or less permanently dependent on others. They lack the ability to restrain their impulses and to exercise control over their own behavior. They become credit problems because their buying is more on the basis of "want" than of "need." They fail to anticipate or to plan for the future. These individuals failed to learn the lessons of responsibility.

Misfortunes and emergencies

Of course, non-payment of bills can arise in certain instances through circumstances which could not reasonably have been anticipated. Sudden illnesses, accidents, and what are called, somewhat impiously, "acts of God," can make it impossible for otherwise well-intentioned and normally prudent persons to fulfill their commitments. These cases, of course, have little to do with socialization and are, by definition, unpredictable.

If the socialization process were not so powerful and usually so successful, it would have been impossible to develop the kind of credit economy we find today. Simply because the procedures and conditions of credit are so widely understood and appreciated and because adherence to a responsible use of credit is so well taught, most collections are màde routinely. The creditor behaves according to certain rules and the customer makes the proper responses.

Use Their Habits to Collect

If the credit granter is to take full advantage of the socialized responses of paying obligations, he should, within limits, adhere to socially prescribed patterns of behavior himself. For example, there are limits to the amount of novelty which may be incorporated in billing forms. If they are too different, they will not be recognized as bills and remittances will not be forthcoming in optimum quantity. If a credit granter wishes to introduce major innovations in his practices, he should be prepared to take the consequences of slower collections until his clientele becomes trained to recognize his invitations to pay. On the other hand, a certain amount of distinctiveness is desirable so that customers may easily discriminate between your bill and other, perhaps less urgent, obligations.

Be methodical

Important matters should be treated as if they were important. Irregular dates for the mailing of bills and slow follow-up of delinquencies are the kinds of behavior which our training has taught us denote unimportant matters. Rigorous attention to a matter indicates its importance. Casual billing procedures invite casual paying habits.

Send a statement

Most consumers expect a statement. Few of them even feel that they are expected to pay on invoice. The carbon copy of a handwritten sales or job ticket is particularly apt to be ignored. The majority of credit business is not handled this way and, therefore, the invoice does not tend to call forth the response of paying.

Watch your timing

The timing of billing is important. Most persons have more or less fixed habits concerning bill-paying. Certain times of the week or month are associated with clearing up debts. These times are usually related to paydays and work schedules. If bills arrive too early, they run a chance of being mislaid. If they arrive too late, they risk being postponed until the next time or of finding funds exhausted. The time of arrival of the statement should be planned to suit the habits of the typical customer. Unfortunately, large credit granters find this difficult for practical reasons. Cycle billing may be desirable from some points of view, but it is not the way to obtain maximum collections. In those cases where cycle billing has improved collections it is probable that prior billing practices were not prompt.

Stress terms

Ideally the new credit customer is informed of the terms at the time his application is approved, in such a manner that he not only understands them but also leaves with the feeling that they are important. Terms are often treated apologetically, as if they were really unimportant to the credit granter. This can be a disservice to the customer. If he gets the impression that the "real" terms, as contrasted with the stated ones, are "at his convenience," it becomes easy for him inadvertently to gain the reputation of being a "slow pay." The terms of payment should be represented as an essential part of the bargain and they should not be hidden by inconspicuous size and style of type on the bill.

Reward promptness

Many credit granters feel that allowing a discount for prompt payment speeds up collections. Others charge a penalty for late payment. There are some indications that, if either is to be used, the discount for prompt payment is more effective than the penalty for delayed payment, and this is in accord with the psychological principles discovered in other areas of human behavior. It is generally true that rewarding desired behavior is more effective than punishing the undesired response.

It is usual for people to pay their bills promptly. A substantial proportion of all accounts is collected routinely. This high degree of uniformity in the behavior of such a diversity of individuals requires explanation. This explanation is provided by an understanding of the process by which individuals learn to become members of a group—the process of socialization. Collection problems arise when the individual learns from a deviant group or when the socialization process fails. The credit granter can increase his collections by making his efforts in the ways which tend to evoke socialized responses in his customers.

KINDS OF COLLECTION PROBLEMS

VI

KINDS OF COLLECTION PROBLEMS

Inevitably, customers will be found who do not follow the rules; cases where collection ceases to be routine. These are the collection problems which require special attention.

Slow Payment

One of the commonest and most annoying of collection problems is caused by lax paying habits. Some individuals seem to remit more or less at their own convenience, frequently taking 60 or 90 days on open accounts or ignoring due dates for installments. These are often good customers otherwise and may ultimately pay. They are a problem because they require reminders and because they consume the time of credit personnel in special handling of their accounts. Some of these casual payers are persons of ample means who feel that their credit is so obviously superior that the creditor should not be concerned about the time of payment. These persons feel that their accounts are "good as gold" anyway. Consequently, no one should be concerned about them. They do not realize that their lack of promptness is an expensive nuisance to those who try to accommodate them.

Other slow payers are slow because they frequently find themselves short of funds. These persons have their budgets stretched tight. When such a person finds himself short of cash for the month, he may sort through his obligations, deciding as he looks at each bill who will get paid now and who will wait. He may send off, for example, his car payment, a rent payment and, then, put the rest aside for next month. There is a hierarchy of urgency in a stack of bills. Individuals can rank their debts in the order in which they personally feel they must be paid. Certain kinds of debts have a high rank in this hierarchy and take precedence in their claims on the customer's funds. Examples of high ranking debts are rent and automobile payments.

Who Gets Paid First

Different obligations acquire their ranks in this hierarchy of bills as the result of a number of factors. Some are ranked higher because of the ease with which the credit granter can act to enforce payment. The threat of termination of service adds to the priority of the utility bill as the possibility of repossession does to the seller of durable goods. Others achieve higher ranking because of a reputation for strict enforcement of payment terms either as a class or as individual firms. Banks and small loan companies derive some of their status in the hierarchy from reputation. The necessity for frequent encounters with the credit granter adds priority to the individual personal loan and, sometimes, to the rent bill. Changes in the hierarchy of obligations can occur as a result of learning.

Although the socialization process is quite effective in teaching the necessity of paying debts, it is not so effective in teaching the necessity of paying them on time. This educational task rests more directly on the credit granters themselves. Unfortunately, many credit granters implicitly go along with the notion that the time of payment is a secondary consideration. Failure to follow up on delinquencies quickly and consistently implies a lack of concern about promptness. Comments like, "Oh, don't send him a bill again this month. Maybe next month he'll be ready to pay it," are too often heard in small credit departments. Other credit granters have effectively advanced the priority of their claims on the customer's current funds.

Teach Prompt Payment

Auto finance companies, for example, have quite deliberately promoted their claims to a high place in the bill-paying hierarchy. They have achieved this with sound psychological techniques designed specifically to impress the debtor with the importance of getting his payment to them on the date due. It is not solely the threat of repossession which has brought the car payment to the top of the heap of bills. Other businesses have the same threat but have not achieved the same status. The urgency rank of the automobile payment is due to training and education.

When an automobile is purchased there is a discussion of terms. The time of the month when payment will be made is the subject of discussion and a specific day of the month is set. If a payment is delayed, a reminder is mailed immediately. New accounts are followed with particular care. If a payment on a new account is delayed, the customer gets a telephone call from the finance company. This practice underlines the concern the company has for punctuality. After the contract is completed and the obligation is paid off, the customer usually receives a credit card which subtly compliments him and serves as a reward for his good behavior. In sending the credit card, the finance company is building for the future. The object is to increase the probability that the next time the customer purchases an automobile he will finance it with them and that he will repeat the behavior of paying his debt on schedule. All these procedures are educationally sound.

Terms—Be specific

Most consumer finance companies train their employees very carefully in methods for concluding loan transactions. Emphasis of payment terms receives specific treatment. Personnel of the loan company are instructed to mention the date payment is due a given number of times and must do so at definite points in the transaction. The borrower is usually impressed with the date on which he is to make his payment by no less than four specific mentions of it in the final minutes of the interview.

Reward payment

When teaching new behavior, the first step is to make it easy for the desired response to occur, to arrange matters so that the behavior you want to teach is probable. This, of course, is done in the discussion of terms and payment dates. When the behavior you want to teach does occur, it should be rewarded. Perhaps the finance companies are missing a bet at this point. Although they usually give a token reward, i.e., a credit card, at the end of the paying sequence, their effectiveness might be increased if they sent some sort of flattering acknowledgement when the first payment is received on time. Other credit granters have done this by sending a form letter which not only tells the customer how much they appreciated his patronage but which also mentions their pleasure at his prompt payment of the account. This reinforces the behavior of prompt payment and makes it more likely to occur the next time he uses his credit or when his next payment is due.

In teaching new behavior it is also important to give attention to the cues which signal to the learner that a certain response is to be made. Here the credit granters of open accounts may have an edge over the finance companies; these credit granters mail a signal (the statement), while most finance companies rely on the debtor to remember with the aid of a payment book. On the other hand, the good finance company employee, in his discussion of payment dates, will usually connect the payment date with some regular or repeated event in the life of the customer, such as payday, and this regular event can then serve as a cue which signals, "Your payment is due now."

Discourage non-payment

When responses other than the one you want to teach occur, that is, being late or not sending in a payment, it is important that there be signals to indicate that this is a wrong response. This signal is the late payment notice or telephone call. It should be more widely used on new accounts by other credit granters. The savings in later collection costs which can be attained by seeing that new customers begin with prompt paying habits will more than compensate for the extra effort involved.

The telephone call can be handled very courteously and diplomatically. One might say, "We have not received your check and we were wondering if we might have made a mistake in your address. We do want to have it right so we can serve you properly." It is probably best not to read the address you have on the account to the customer and have him verify it. This more or less forces him to admit that he received your statement. You can ask for his address and state that you will check your mailing list to be sure that it appears that way. You can then close with, "In the meantime, Mr. Doe, your balance is $19.98. May we expect your check for that amount?"

From a psychological point of view, many things other than credit cards or complimentary letters may be rewards. Social approval, as in the complimentary letter, is certainly an important reward, but so, too, is a pleasant taste sensation, relief from hunger, relief from thirst, or relief from tension, anxiety and fear. When a debtor finds himself short of funds and sorts through his obligations, he is usually upset and more or less anxious. If he gets relief from this anxiety by skipping your bill, he is learning to skip your bill. This is one important reason why a prompt reminder is necessary. The reminder is both a signal indicating that he has made a "wrong" response and a gentle punishment for having done so.

Let Them Know the Rules

Some companies fear to attempt such a program of education with their customers. They fear they will arouse antagonism and lose customers if they follow such a strict credit policy and, indeed, this is a possibility. They fear that, if they indicate that they truly *do* care when customers pay their bills, a great migration to competitors will follow. It is doubtful that a great many desirable credit customers would be lost as a result of gradually tightening up your collection policy. The great majority, the prompt payment customers, would not have occasion to learn that there had been a change. Most of the others would accept it as a matter of course. The few who become indignant can be handled with tact.

Be consistent

In your behavior toward your credit customers you are constantly teaching them what to expect of you on the next encounter. If you have followed a credit policy which failed to take exception to delays in payment, your customers may have taken this failure as permission to continue the practice. You have taught them to believe that time of payment is not important. In your behavior you have established the ground rules for the game and your customers are merely taking advantage of their privileges under the rules. If your customers have been taught in this fashion, they might feel that a sudden change in policy was equivalent to changing the rules in the middle of the game. An abrupt switch could very well generate resentment and a feeling that you had been unfair. If established customers are to be retrained, the program must proceed in stages. New credit customers may be more immediately indoctrinated with the new rules.

It's a privilege

Credit is not only a convenience, but the possession of charge privileges still carries some connotation of status and prestige. The status attaching to charge privileges at different establishments is partly a function of the selectivity which the establishment exercises in its choice of credit customers. Selectivity of customers is usually accompanied by a more rigid insistence on terms. The prestige value of an account may be used in selling the policy to customers. For example, this approach can be used: "Yes, Mrs. Customer, our policy is perhaps stricter. That is why we are somewhat more selective in our credit customers. We try only to accept persons like you who are able to meet our higher standards." Certainly there is no reason to be ashamed of being definite about terms. If the customer were letting you use his money, he would want to know when he would get it back. It is possible to be firm without being unpleasant.

It is firm

It may seem strange, but there is a certain feeling of security for the customer if the terms are definite. If the necessity to meet an obligation at a certain time is perceived as inevitable, there is less temptation to take chances. One feels somehow safer driving an automobile in a familiar town where one knows the rules than in an unfamiliar town where one not only does not know the rules but also does not know how rigorously they are enforced. Some financial obligations are seldom a matter for consideration; they are met automatically. One gambles on the consequences of ignoring other bills.

Watch for overbuying

Irregular paying habits may also develop as a result of overbuying. In some instances the account grows to a size which the customer feels he cannot handle in one payment. Or, his payments grow to a total he cannot handle with one paycheck. He may then pay only a portion of the amount due, but during the next month he continues to buy. He is then once more unable to meet his obligations in full. If the cycle is allowed to continue he will find himself rather hopelessly mired. At some point he must reduce his spending. It is highly important that this situation be detected quickly and action taken. The creditor must realize that he is not only competing against other creditors for a customer's current funds, but he is also competing with the insistent sales efforts of those who would sell him more. Such a customer not only has other debts, but he also has wants for new goods and services. The psychologist calls this a conflict situation. The customer finds himself torn between two or more opposing motives. His situation is simply, "If I pay this, I won't have money for that."

When they want to pay, but can't

On the one hand he is impelled to pay you and on the other hand he does not want to. He will do so only if one of two things happens. Either his motives for paying must become stronger than the resistances, or his resistances must be weakened. The resistances to paying may be reduced by a variety of things, e.g., getting an income tax refund, finding a place to get a loan, or receiving a raise. The motivations for paying may increase as a result of increased guilt, increased anxiety, or a desire to get credit for more goods.

In retail sales there is another situation in which the overbuying is more apparent than real. The behavior is similar, but the causes are different. This is the case of a wife who has exceeded her real or implied budget and who is reluctant to let her husband find out about the situation. Since funds are presumably available in the family coffers, the goal is to obtain payment without causing a family squabble. In handling such a problem, it may be expedient to hint to the wife diplomatically that the husband may be contacted. You could suggest that, after all, it is really the husband's credit rating which is at stake and, since this is the case, perhaps you should be discussing the matter with him. If the wife is still afraid to face the situation with her husband, you should consider actually talking with the husband.

Emergencies

Some individuals become delinquent in their payments as a result of unavoidable emergencies in their lives. The sensible and human thing to do in such cases is to work out some payment plan with the customer. There is a tendency to go overboard in such situations. Certainly it is all right to express sympathy, but, if one does not wish to be the last repaid when the crisis is past, he should not give the impression that the granting of extensions or the arrangement of terms is a routine matter. Be courteous and be considerate, but do not be casual. The customer is learning from your attitude, and, if he learns that extensions can be obtained easily in emergencies, he may learn to have numerous emergencies.

Arrangements for terms

Be serious about arrangements and be definite about them. You should not accept an arrangement which includes such provisions as, "When I get on my feet again," or "As soon as I get back to work." You should ask, "When do you think that will be?" Explain that you have to have a date in order to set up your tickler file, to mark your records, etc. At least get a commitment as to the time when the customer will do something.

Some customers defend their delay in payment with the excuse that an adjustment is pending. In such cases it is important to find out just how much money is involved in the adjustment. If the adjustment does not involve the entire balance, you should ask that the customer send payment for the remainder which is not in dispute.

Collection problems occur in great variety and cannot be entirely eliminated. They can be minimized through proper education of credit customers and intelligent far-sighted treatment of those problems which arise.

COLLECTION STRATEGY

VII

COLLECTION STRATEGY

In order to keep control of the collection effort and to plan strategy for collecting, it is necessary to be informed about the flow of collections.

One of the most effective methods to obtain this information is by means of age analysis. In its simplest form, age analysis is simply a listing of the accounts receivable in columns according to the months in which purchases were made or services rendered. This is merely a device for keeping track of the amount of money outstanding and the period for which it has been outstanding. For the small credit granter who grants credit only on a straight 30-day charge basis, the form published by the National Retail Credit Association may be convenient. For those larger credit granters who offer such plans as the revolving charge account and the optional credit plan, the problem is more complicated. Although accounting methods are outside the scope of this book, proper handling of delinquent accounts depends upon bringing to light those which require special handling. Some procedure for aging is essential for this purpose.

Keep Track of the Age of Your Accounts

When an account has passed through the routine reminders and has not been paid, it deserves special consideration. An individual approach needs to be taken. In order that an individual approach may be applied, it is necessary to insititute procedures which will separate those accounts which demand attention from the routine accounts. Although this need may seem obvious, it is a fact that even some large credit granters do not have an adequate automatic detection system for past due accounts. An account may pass through the routine collection effort, there may be no prescribed next step, and the account may languish in the files until such time as the "tub," ledger, or what-have-you is periodically examined and the delinquent accounts noted. This can occur a considerable length of time after the last routine step has been taken, with resultant damage to the account's ultimate collectibility.

Why Account Age Is Important

The decline in the collectibility of accounts as they grow older is partly due to the mobility of our population. People change residence and may fail to leave forwarding addresses. Even if they leave forwarding addresses, mail is delayed in reaching them. Sometimes it goes astray and does not reach them at all. Unless you can find your customer and ask him for your money, you may not get it.

As time passes, the value of goods or services received earlier diminishes. The three-month-old stove no longer has quite the sparkle it had when it was first purchased. The new dress can already be torn or stained. The contrast between the present value of the money required to pay the account and that of the dress can make it difficult for the customer to part with the money. As a matter of fact, after the lapse of a number of months, one can begin to feel it was a foolish purchase to begin with. From here it is only a step to blaming the creditor (faulty memories make this easier) for pressuring one into making the original purchase.

The fact that accounts receivable decline in value as a function of age is well known. Table 1 shows the erosion of accounts receivable as a function of age.

Table 1

AVERAGE DECLINE IN VALUE WITH AGE

Months Past Due	*Percentage Loss*
3	10
4	14
5	19
6	37
12	58
24	74
36	83

If the 90-day account, for which each dollar has already shrunk to 90 cents, is allowed to rest for another 90 days, the value declines to 67 cents on the dollar.

The rate of depreciation is greatest during this three-month period. Clearly, prompt action is needed at the 90-day point to forestall this accelerating loss of value.

Account Age for Three Goals

The action to be taken is determined by an analysis of the individual account and a clear understanding of the goals to be accomplished. These goals are:

(1) to obtain payment in accordance with terms,
(2) to maintain the patronage and good will of the customers, and
(3) to keep credit losses at a minimum.

1. *Obtaining compliance with terms*

Obtaining payment is not, in itself, a complete job. If, on future balances, the customer again is a credit problem, the issue has only been delayed. Ideally, the collection effort should educate the customer to comply with terms in the future. This task can be approached best if the collector understands why the account happened to become delinquent. If, as it may well be, the cause is that the customer is not impressed with the importance of prompt payment, a tactful explanation of credit customs may solve the problem. On the other hand, if the delay was due to some unfortunate circumstances, an expression of sympathy can be followed with the suggestion that the customer notify you in the future when circumstances arise which make delays necessary. In your effort to assure that future payments will be made in accordance with terms, be courteous and pleasant, but leave no chance for misunderstanding. Do not make it necessary for the customer to infer your meaning; state it clearly. If you *can* be misunderstood you probably *will* be.

2. *Keeping good will*

Maintaining the patronage and good will of customers can be incompatible with your first goal, but it is not necessarily so. You can be insistent and firm without giving offense. To do so, of course, requires tact and finesse, but tact and finesse come more easily if your attitude is right.

As a collector you have a job to do in order that the company you represent can continue to serve its customers, provide income for its employees, and compensate its owners for the investment they have made. While you may personally sympathize, you have no choice but to observe the rules and to insist that, if the customer is to enjoy the privileges of credit, he accept the responsibilities as well.

It is unfortunate when the actions of individuals lead them to suffer physical injuries, but the consequences are not mitigated by the virtue or good intentions of the person involved. No one feels that the law of gravity should be repealed when he drops a hammer on his toe. Although the consequences of carelessness in economic matters may not be quite as direct or inevitable as in the physical area, the principles which prescribe these consequences are sound. The misfortune of one individual does not legitimatize injustice to others. Our social structure provides institutions both for loans and for charity. Neither the open account nor the installment credit contract is designed to meet these needs. When a customer uses this kind of credit arrangement to secure financing for other wants, or worse, to obtain charity, he is doing an injustice to those who depend on the credit-granting company for income or services. A realistic understanding of these facts will help in developing the kind of attitude which can combine firmness with understanding.

3. *Keeping losses at a minimum*

The third goal—that of keeping credit losses at a minimum—must be interpreted within the framework of credit policy. The goal is to strive for the minimum loss possible at the risk level which has been set. There is more to it than collecting past due bills and closing bad debt accounts. Minimizing credit losses involves recognizing an unprofitable account and doing something constructive about it. Briefly, the unprofitable account is one on which the expenses of handling exceed the expected return.

a. *Low Dollar Volume.* An account may be unprofitable simply because of low dollar volume. The customer may not do enough business with you to justify the trouble of keeping his account on the books. Either the customer should be sold on making the account profitable, or, if this is impossible, the account should become inactive. Many alert credit granters make periodic mailings to individuals whose accounts are not being used. In these mailings, they note that the account is not being used, they ask if there is something wrong, they invite use of the account, and they sometimes offer inducements for greater use. Perhaps a later mailing could explain the necessity of closing the account with an invitation to reopen it if the customer should need such a convenience in the future.

In making mailings to these accounts it is useful to use envelopes which request the post office to furnish a Form 3547. You will then be notified by the post office of any changes of address which your customers have listed with their local post office. These changes may enable you to eliminate accounts which will obviously not be used. In all cases, when an account is closed or made inactive, it is good public relations to send an appropriate letter.

b. *Excessive Adjustments.* An account may be unprofitable because of excessive adjustments or returns of merchandise. Some customers view a charge account as a means to receive goods on approval; virtually all their purchases are conditional. And, because most stores follow a liberal return and adjustment policy, the customer may not realize that there is any limit to the privilege. If such a misapprehension exists, the customer is not totally to blame. These accounts require the utmost in diplomacy and a keen sensitivity to the feelings of the other person. Naturally these problems should be handled through conversation, not by letter, and preferably through personal interview. In most cases an honest statement of your dilemma and an appeal for help is the best procedure. It is essential that your comments avoid any suggestion of reproach.

c. *Special Handling.* An account may be unprofitable because it repeatedly requires special handling. The general principles involved in attempting to educate slow payers have already been discussed. If these efforts fail, consideration should be given to closing the account.

Evaluating the Delinquent Account

1. *Amount owed*

With the goals of the collection campaign firmly in mind, the account should be evaluated. You would first consider the amount owed. It is evident that a company can afford to devote more time and effort to the collection of large balances than it can to smaller ones. Two mistakes come easily in this connection, and credit men often make both. It is possible to be too willing to write off small balances as uncollectible. Small balances add up to large sums. A more common error is to pursue collection efforts too far. Perhaps this is the more common error because of the pressure to maintain a low loss ratio.

However, either mistake can lead to an unprofitable operation, the former through direct credit losses and the latter through a more insidious rise in the costs of recovery. The time to terminate collection efforts is crucial. Your decision can make or lose money.

The amount owed has a further significance, however. Regardless of how the size of the account compares with your company's average past due balance, or whether you, personally, see it as a little or a lot, for the purposes of your collection strategy the most important issue is how the customer sees the amount. You should ask yourself whether the amount involved is large or small with respect to his apparent ability to pay. If a customer is reluctant to part with an amount which could be taken from one week's income without causing undue hardship, you may suspect his motives. In general, the larger the income, the larger is the proportion of it which is discretionary, that is, can be spent as he chooses. From the average wage earner with, for example, a weekly pay of 75 dollars, other things being equal, you should be able to get as much as 35 dollars in one payment. As the income rises, there is not only more left after the basic costs of subsistence have been met, but there is more room to maneuver funds, to delay this or omit that in order to satisfy the more insistent creditors.

2. *How long delinquent*

You should consider the length of time the account has been delinquent. As was mentioned earlier, the value of accounts receivable falls rapidly as a function of time. The longer the money has been owed, the smaller are your chances of collecting. The most rapid rate of erosion occurs between the third and the sixth month, flattening out to a fairly steady rate of loss after one year. This period, when your accounts are suffering the greatest percentage loss, is the most important period for close attention.

3. *Pattern of payment*

The pattern of delinquency is also important. You should note whether there have been token or part payments. Were they substantial? Did the total balance owed increase or shrink during the period of delinquency? The significance of part payments is judged by the size of the balance and the customer's ability to pay. The question to be resolved is whether the customer's behavior reflects a sincere attempt to take care of his obligation or whether it is only an attempt to appease you. However, if there is sincerity in effort, there should also be some tangible result. The total balance should not be growing. Sincerity does not pay debts. It is altogether possible to build the foundations for financial disaster with a mortar of good intentions.

4. *New or old customer*

How long has the account been on your books? If it is a new account, you have a responsibility to make your policy clear. Neglecting a delinquency at this point is serving notice of a lenient credit policy. A polite reminder can often prevent future troubles by making the rules clear at the beginning of the game. If it is an old account, you would want to know if delinquencies have occurred frequently in the past. A repeated pattern of delayed payment requires a different approach from one appropriate for a first instance of delinquency in an account with a long record of prompt payment. The repeated pattern poses a problem of retraining. The isolated instance may be the clue to a complaint, or it may merely be the rare occasion of a statement going astray. In the first case, you may have the opportunity to salvage a customer. In the second, your concern, politely expressed, advertises your thoroughness.

5. *Previous handling*

As you study the history of an account you should also examine any notations about pending adjustments. Ask yourself how the customer has followed through on any previous promises. Does he honor his commitments? You should be sure to note whether the account is one which had previously been closed and re-opened. Why was it closed before? Should it have been reopened? Is this one which should be pressed for payment quickly?

At this point you should have developed some ideas about the customer and the tactics appropriate to the problem he poses. These ideas should be tentative. Your strategy should be flexible. No matter how thoroughly you have examined the data available to you, it is important to remember that you *may* have gotten a false picture. Your approach must remain flexible so as to permit changes in it as new information comes in. If you erred in your original estimate, or if you devised the wrong strategy, be quick to change to a better one. Because one procedure has been successful in a number of situations does not mean it is the best for all. Keep the objectives of your campaign in mind so that you neither become tied up in methods and techniques nor find yourself repeating a stereotyped ritual.

In order to give intelligent attention to past due accounts, you must have a method for drawing your attention to those which are getting old. With respect to accounts receivable, time is a dollar-eater. Older accounts are more difficult to collect, and you will collect fewer of them. In your attention to these past due accounts, however, you will do well to remember that whatever course you decide upon should be considered in terms of three goals. The goals are (1) to promote future compliance with terms, (2) to keep good will, and (3) to control losses. You will find it easier to accomplish these goals if your action is preceded by a thorough analysis of the account in which you weigh such factors as the time past due, the pattern of payment, the amount due, the time the customer has been on the books, and any previous experience you have had with that customer.

COLLECTION BY MAIL

VIII

COLLECTION BY MAIL

Communication through the mail has certain characteristics which should be appreciated if collection efforts by this medium are to be most effective. The whole sequence of receiving, opening and reading a letter or mailing piece is distinctively different from a conversation, either vis-a-vis or by telephone. The features which distinguish this mode of communication from others may, in some situations, be used to advantage in the collection effort. The same features may be quite disadvantageous in others. Although many of these differences are more or less obvious, a conscious recognition of them is desirable so that they may be used to advantage when that is possible, and, also so that pitfalls may be avoided.

Six Characteristics of Collection by Mail

1. *Less insistent and more polite*

No matter what the content of an envelope may be, it is less insistent in its demand for immediate attention than is the ringing of a telephone or the presence of another person. A letter does not have to be opened now, and, if opened, it does not have to be read now. A letter can be rather easily ignored. Its reading may be postponed. Mail does not interrupt. It may be handled at a convenient time. Because of these characteristics, mail usually is both less urgent and more polite.

2. *Time for response*

The recipient of a letter is not under pressure to react immediately. He has time for reflection and planning. His response to the message can be considered. Whatever the response to a letter may be, it is less likely to be spontaneous than would be the reply to the same message communicated orally. Despite glaring exceptions, the reaction to a mail message is generally more reasoned, more calculated, and more rational. Even when a reply is abusive and emotional in its tone, you can assume that more thought entered into the composition than the same person would have given to a scathing oral retort.

3. *Lacks spontaneous feedback*

When you send a letter you do not get the same quick and responsive feedback as when you speak to an individual. You cannot be so sure of the real emotional impact of your message. You are not present when it is read and you must, therefore, use a less individualized approach. Your message and your style are custom-made for the generalized customer, the typical person, rather than tailored for a specific one. You must assume that the one who receives your communication will react in the usual way.

4. *More formal and impersonal*

Partly as a result of the lack of an immediate feedback, most written communications are more circumspect in their phrasing. They rely less on the inferences of the receiver. The words have to carry their meaning without the help of intonation or inflection. Letters rely more on the formal aspects of communication. Complete sentences are used. Sentence follows sentence with more logical connection, and ideas are grouped in a more coherent pattern. Written communications are more formal and more impersonal. Although the personality of the writer may show through in a written message, his personality is muted and subordinated to the content.

5. *Greater finality*

Somehow, the written word often has the connotation of greater finality than does the spoken word. There is more of a feeling that what is written is without recall. Often, too, the written word has an aura of legality which is illustrated in the common remark, "Would you put that in writing?" What is written is felt to be binding to a greater extent than what is merely spoken. This characteristic should be kept in mind when one is tempted to make a specific promise or a threat in a collection letter or notice. Unless you can and will follow it through punctiliously, leave it out.

6. *Less social*

All in all, there is a vast difference in the background of experience which individuals have had in their dealings with words which were experienced through the eye and those which were experienced through the ear. Oral communications have generally been interpersonal and social. They have been associated with dealings with other people and they evoke the kinds of reactions which have been learned in social contexts. Experiences with written words have been more in learning situations and school associations. They are more private and more solitary.

Why Mail Is Best for the First Effort

Politeness, impersonality, and appeal to the typical customer should characterize the initial collection effort. Mail is the medium of choice for the early phases of the collection effort.

Statements sent by mail are standard procedure for routine collections. At the time the first statement is sent, there is, presumably, no need for urgency, one does not require any feedback, and the relationship with the customer calls for courtesy and a degree of formality. Mail is ideal for the purpose, and most accounts are collected by this simple and relatively inexpensive means.

The Most Important Collection Tool—The Statement

From the point of view of sheer volume, the statement is the most important of all collection tools. It carries so much of the collection load that it deserves more attention than it usually gets. Probably it gets less attention than it merits because most people pay their bills regardless of how the statement is rendered. Some individuals would telephone you even if you did not send a statement at all. More, of course, will pay if you do send a statement, and even more will pay if you give attention to how the statement is rendered. Any statement gets a large response. Improvements will usually only increase effectiveness by a few percentage points. But, even a small increase in the effectiveness of this first piece of collection mail can reduce later collection problems and greatly lessen costs. You should take care that your statement does the very best job possible.

1. *It Is a Request for Payment.* Basically, the statement is a communication to the customer. Although a copy may perform a service for the accounting department, this function should remain distinctly secondary. The statement is a request for payment. Although this request is seldom phrased in words, the customer understands the message. He has learned what the statement means. It is a symbol which has become an accepted part of our credit structure, and, if it looks enough like a statement, the meaning is readily interpreted.

There are two other things the statement should explicitly communicate to the customer and which should be spelled out. You should tell him clearly how much he owes and for what he owes.

2. *It Should Tell Him How Much He Owes.* The amount which the customer is expected to pay should be absolutely clear and unambiguous. If calculations are necessary, these calculations should have been done for the customer, and the amount due should be clearly indicated on the statement. With rotating credit plans, or with other complex credit arrangements, this requirement may pose problems of procedure, but collections will suffer if the customer is expected to divide by five, multiply by a decimal, or even to remember a flat monthly payment.

Calculations take time. For many persons arithmetic is distasteful. Both the need for time and the dislike for figuring build small resistances to making payment. Little resistances may not be important for those persons who are highly motivated to pay, but for the marginal ones just a little resistance may make the difference between paying and not paying.

Even more important than the resistance to arithmetic is the widespread lack of arithmetical competence. The ability of your customers to do simple arithmetic is probably at a much lower level than you suppose. A large proportion of our population is simply unable to compute percentages. Many persons have trouble with division, and accurate multiplication is far from common. Not only can your bookkeeping and personnel departments verify these facts from bitter experience, but evidence is available from other sources. For example, in a college class composed entirely of graduate students and upperclassmen, a majority failed to pass an eighth grade arithmetic test even though they had previously been warned that it was a requirement of the course. If college seniors and graduate students cannot do arithmetic at the eighth grade level, you should not expect too much from your average customer.

Past balances, payments made during the month, and other credits, if included, should be clear. Do not leave the burden of interpreting some complex financial document up to the customer. If, perhaps in the interests of cost reduction, you are sending a copy of your ledger page as a statement, be sure that the one entry on that ledger page which represents the amount you expect your customer to send or bring to you can be identified as such without difficulty. Give him a total balance due that is payable now and label it as such.

Current billing procedures in consumer credit have evolved from prior procedures in mercantile credit and with personal credit to individuals of substance. Too many of these procedures implicitly assume a knowledge of business affairs and practices which is not justified when dealing with the general population which is involved in consumer credit today. Probably relatively few of your statements are going to persons who are well versed in business procedures and practices. Your statement should be prepared for the average individual, not the businessman.

3. *The Bill Should Itemize.* Your statement should tell the customer what he is being billed for. The statement should itemize the goods or services rendered for which payment is due, and this should be in terms which are comprehensible to the one from whom payment is expected. Abbreviations and terms which are easily understood in your business may be only so much gibberish to customers. Catalog numbers may be efficient for your accounting department, but they are hardly an explanation for the customer. If the customer has forgotten and there is any question about an item, the bill may be put aside. Once put aside, it is easy to delay or to postpone payment further. The customer wants to know what he is paying for before he pays. You would do well to tell him without making him ask.

Failure to itemize services is quite often found among professional men who frequently follow the tradition of having a printed statement reading only, "For professional services." It is true that the nature of these professional services cannot always be expressed in terms which will be understood by the lay person, but it is possible to list dates of consultations and for whom the services were rendered.

If your itemization consists of sales slips attached to the statement, be sure that they are legible. Also, watch your abbreviations. While "bra B 36" may be perfectly comprehensible to your sales clerk, the gentleman who is expected to pay the bill may not be knowledgeable in such matters.

Make It Easy to Pay

If you want maximum collections, you must make it as easy as possible for the customer to make payment when he opens your bill or when he settles down to write checks or goes to obtain money orders. You can make this job easier for him in many ways.

You can certainly enclose a self-addressed envelope. It is generally recognized that enclosing a return envelope with the statement increases routine collections by a significant percentage. It is strange that the practice is not more general. If balances are small, the difference in effectiveness between the postage paid return envelope and the one which requires the customer to provide his own stamp may not justify the added cost of the former. These differences in effectiveness can easily be tested by the individual credit granter who can then adopt the procedure which gives the best results for his operation.

You can be sure that your address appears on the statement so that the customer knows where to mail his remittance. You should include city and state in that address and be sure that the address on the statement is the same as the one on the envelope you include. If the statement has one address and the return envelope another, you will not only receive remittances at two addresses, but you will also confuse many of your customers. If you have several divisions, as do some oil companies, customers may be receiving statements from more than one division and may get their remittances confused.

If your statement is of two parts, one part of which is to be returned with the remittance, be certain to include your address on the part which is to be returned. Your customer may discard his portion of the statement before he addresses the envelope. If you use such a format, your firm name would be best included on both portions. The itemized record to be retained is of little use unless there is some way of identifying the company or person to whom it was paid. Also, with the two-part statement, take care to have the portion you want returned separated from the itemized portion by perforations so that the payor may conveniently separate the parts.

You can make payment easier by printing your statements in a size that can be conveniently slipped into a number six envelope, the size most people use for paying bills. This should be possible with one easy fold at the most. Certainly they should not be of a size which can only be contained in a large envelope and they should not require accordion pleats or other fancy folding in order to stuff them into the envelope.

If you include a return envelope, by all means insure that the return portion of your statement fits into it easily. Remember, you also want a payment, so make your return envelope of a height which will contain a wide check. Currency exchanges and banks issue checks wider than the personalized miniature varieties currently fashionable.

Business machine cards do not easily fit into envelopes without folding. If you want the card returned intact you must design and include a return envelope for the purpose. Otherwise, you should have the card designed so that only a portion must accompany the remittance.

No discussion of specific instances can cover all of the mistakes which can be made in designing a statement. However, if the credit granter will keep in mind the very basic fact that the statement is prepared for the customer, he will be less apt to create new blunders. The statement is a request for payment. It must be understandable and simple. Everything must be arranged to make it as easy as possible for the customer to remit.

After the Statement, What?

If, despite a very conscientious attention to the customer, you fail to collect with the original statement, you would normally send another statement after a certain grace period. Custom has set this period as 30 days in most circumstances. Ideally, this statement should *not* be identical with the first. Although it need not contain any special message, the fact that it is not the initial and routine statement should be apparent. You can create this feeling of distinctiveness through color, type, format, or the use of identifying words and phrases. The second statement could be on colored paper, could use ink of a different color, could be set in bolder type, or could be labelled "Second Statement," "Sixty Day Notice," or simply have a large number two printed in the corner. The object of doing this is to convey the fact that the customer's delay has been noticed. If one is being watched, his behavior is usually more conformist than if he is unnoticed.

Let us now suppose that the 30-day grace period has passed and that you have sent your second statement. What should be the next step? The use of a special letter at this point in the collection campaign is probably both unnecessary and undesirable. After all, up to now, you have communicated only the fact that you have noted the customer's delay. You have expressed no concern over the matter. Your next goal is again to remind him of his obligation, to let him again know that you are aware of his delay, but this time you want to express a degree of concern about the matter. Still, you want the whole business to appear somewhat impersonal. There are various ways to get this message across.

Some credit granters send a third statement. This fails to communicate concern. Some use a rubber stamp on a statement. Even if the text of the stamp is well composed, the method itself seems a little abrupt. Most include a printed insert with a statement. The growing practice of mailing advertising inserts with statements may diminish the effectiveness of this procedure. The customer may mistake the insert for advertising and fail to notice its contents. Still other credit granters attach a printed sticker to a statement. This method is fairly effective in many cases, but it is rather laborious when large numbers of delinquent notices must be sent. Stickers with a wide variety of messages are available from a number of sources. The best procedure is probably to use a notice which is specially designed for the purpose. This notice, since some impersonality is still to be preserved, might be titled "Past Due Statement," or "Delayed Payment Notice." This action has a slightly higher degree of urgency and indicates a higher level of concern.

Develop Urgency

The atmosphere of urgency and concern constitutes a major variable in the collection campaign. The sequence of collection efforts normally proceeds in an orderly fashion from the routine statement through intermediate stages to a final ultimatum or legal process. The pace at which this atmosphere of urgency is developed profoundly affects collections. You may vary this pace according to the medium of the appeal (written or oral), the content of your message, and its timing. We have already seen that the written appeal is usually felt to be less urgent and demanding than the oral, and we have used written means to create a moderate feeling of urgency. In the initial phases of the collection sequence the pace at which successive appeals increase in urgency hinges on collection policy. In later appeals the increments can be individually determined. In either case they may be manipulated by the collector if he knows what he is doing.

Urgency Demands Timing

Timing is an essential determinant of urgency. Credit custom dictates the grace period between the first and second statements. This interval is more or less fixed by the practices current in your area of business. You have more latitude for maneuver in the timing of subsequent appeals for payment. The less the interval between them, the greater is the demanding tone. Although no specific interval can be recommended for every credit granter, it may be said that there is a widespread tendency to err on the side of generosity. Most credit granters allow too much time to elapse before the first reminder and between subsequent ones.

The argument for longer intervals is usually one of billing procedure. Those who wait longer plead that shorter intervals put too much burden on the billing department, that it is not feasible to send notices more frequently, and that crossing in the mail of payments and statements creates a problem. Those who do send notices more frequently attest to a better collection flow and deny that crossing of remittances and notices is a problem.

It is felt that most credit granters allow too much time to elapse before the first reminder and between subsequent ones. The decision concerning this procedure must, of course, be affected by the nature of your business, your clientele, and your credit policy. Nevertheless, unless there are compelling reasons for selecting a longer period, it is recommended that neither interval exceed 15 days.

The Crucial Stage

Assuming that the account has received the treatment recommended here, what is its status now? Thirty days, more or less, elapsed before the routine statement. Another 30 passed before a second statement was sent and another 15 before the first notice. You have waited another 15 days and the account is now 90 days old. This is a crucial point. Despite anything the individual credit granter can do, a widespread feeling exists that "ninety days is cash." Although you may have spelled out your terms clearly, the customer may feel still that he has a full 90-day stretch. So long as such a feeling prevails it is risky to increase the urgency of your tone too abruptly at this point. A written procedure is still indicated, but what should it be?

Again, the answer has to be an individual one, tailored to the needs of your particular operation. Many persons recommend using a different sticker or another statement insert. However, the sticker or insert has already failed once. A change of tactic is probably better. Further, change commands attention. This appeal should be distinctive. Also, since it is our contention that there is a bias to build urgency too slowly, it is recommended that this message go in letter form. But, it should not be individually typed.

The individually typed letter is not only more expensive, but it also is more personal. We should still preserve some flavor of impersonality at the 90-day stage. The letter may be either printed or reproduced by some other means. The phrasing should be courteous and should include a face-saving device for the customer. In fact, all collection letters up to the very end of the internal collection process should permit some way for the customer to preserve his pride and self-esteem.

Help the Customer Preserve His Pride

There are three commonly used devices for achieving this purpose. You may suggest (1) that perhaps your previous notices have been overlooked, (2) that payment is in the mail, or (3) that an adjustment is pending. The phrasing of these excuses offered to the customer can be varied almost infinitely. They should be included in the early notices and letters. Later notices and letters should not exclude the possibility of an excuse. Every person wants to maintain a good opinion of himself and you can afford to allow this privilege if you can get your money and keep a customer. Do not forget, though, to include a request for the money. In composing such a letter, do not allow yourself to become so intent on avoiding embarrassment for the customer that you fail to communicate this primary message.

When the 90-day letter has been sent, the account has passed the stage of routine treatment. At this point it deserves individual scrutiny and attention. Subsequent tactics should be dictated by an analysis of the account in question.

Whether you should proceed quickly to build an atmosphere of greater urgency or develop the atmosphere more deliberately depends on this analysis. If it is felt that the matter should proceed slowly, perhaps additional letters are indicated. On the other hand, if the customer was a marginal risk to begin with, you may wish to accelerate the tempo. You may wish to consider the possibility of sending a telegram or a special delivery letter. Both of these devices carry a distinct appeal of urgency. In any event you should have a complete assortment of form letters on hand to meet your needs.

Why Use Form Letters?

Emphasis has been placed on the form letter because there is some research to indicate that the additional effectiveness of the individually typed letter is not worth the difference in cost. This finding may very well not apply in some credit operations. Certainly credit granters who deal in large balances would want to test the proposition for themselves.

In using mail for collection the matter of cost is quite important. The expense of sending letters is not immediately apparent. Studies which have been done on the cost of sending individually dictated and typed letters vary in their conclusions, but the cost is high according to all of them. Uniformly, they conclude that each letter costs in excess of a dollar, and some find the cost per letter closer to two dollars. Certainly this kind of expense cannot be incurred indiscriminately.

Those credit granters who feel that they must use individually prepared letters should give some consideration to machines which type letters automatically from prepared texts. They might also consider paragraph dictation as a device to minimize cost. In order to use paragraph dictation, it is first necessary to compose and assemble a number of paragraphs covering most situations encountered. The dictator then merely indicates to the typist which of these paragraphs should be copied and in what order. Even with paragraph dictation there is a considerable amount of time consumed in making decisions, and decision-making time is usually expensive.

Whether the collection letter is individually typed from a prepared text or is a form letter, it has two additional advantages over the individually composed letter. Since it has been written at leisure, it is less likely to contain anything which could inadvertently offend the customer and damage public relations, and it is less likely to provide a basis for legal action against you by those who are litigiously inclined. This point, of course, has a converse. The person who is to dictate collection letters should be highly trained and capable of avoiding both damage to public relations and legal pitfalls.

Form Letters for Frequent Situations

In addition to form letters which specifically request payment, most credit granters find that they need other form letters designed to deal with recurrent credit problems—the special situations. For example, all who do business on credit encounter the problem of the bad check. For most, this problem arises with sufficient regularity to make individual handling expensively inefficient. A routine letter to the drawer of the check calling his attention to the matter will clear up most of these situations. However, it is not infrequently found that a replacement check will be sent to you which, in its turn, will also "bounce." You may find it expedient, in your bad check letter, specifically to suggest that you would like a money order or a cashier's check. This will not eliminate all of the repeaters, but a significant proportion will comply with your request.

There are a number of other special situations which may deserve form letters because of their frequency of occurrence. These situations may be discovered by an analysis of the problems which are covered by your correspondence. Although the needs of credit granters are different, some situations are fairly common. There is the case of the customer who buys on an account which has been closed. Some may order from you but have not opened an account. Women customers may marry and change their names without advising you. You will inevitably receive payments and be unable to identify the account to which the payment should apply. Form letters should be available to handle the majority of these situations routinely so that only the exceptions require individual decisions and special handling.

The collection program which has been recommended includes four routine steps followed by individual attention. The routine steps are:

30 days	Original statement
60 days	Distinctive second statement
75 days	Past due notice
90 days	Collection letter

At 97 days you should give the account individual attention. Take care throughout the routine steps that you make it easy for the customer to remit. You should have available an adequate variety of form letters and notices both for the special collection effort which follows the routine phase and for handling ordinary collection problems.

CONSTRUCTION OF LETTERS AND NOTICES

IX

CONSTRUCTION OF LETTERS AND NOTICES

If your letters and notices are to have their greatest effect, you should devote considerable care to their construction. Both the phrasing of your appeal and the form in which that appeal is conveyed can affect the results you obtain. Letters and notices are expensive to produce, expensive to mail, and the difference in the money collected by good ones as contrasted with poor ones can be substantial in amount. Form letters and notices deserve your thoughtful attention. There are some principles which you can observe to make it more likely that your mail will produce the intended result.

Eight Characteristics in Effective Letter Construction

1. *Be brief*

Your message, after all, is essentially simple; you want payment now. The remainder of your content is either sugar-coating for this message or an appeal for action. Long exhortations to action tend to bore rather than to stimulate. Lengthy and verbose attention to the customer's feelings can easily begin to sound like an apology, and you should not apologize for requesting what is due. Such honeyed phrases as, "When one of our valued customers lets his account run a trifle beyond the due date. . . ," have the ring of insincerity. You can be tactful and polite without being wordy.

2. *Leave the customer an "out"*

Second, as mentioned before, allow the customer to save face. Either offer him a convenient excuse for his delay, such as overlooking payment, or leave the way open for such a plausible explanation.

3. *Tell him how much*

Always specify the amount of money you want. Do not make it necessary for the customer to dig through his papers to find out how much he should send. This practice not only makes it convenient for him to pay you, but also keeps the amount in his mind. Often, he would like to forget it.

4. *Tell him what to do*

Suggest a definite action for the customer to take. Do not assume that he will mail a remittance simply because you mention that the account is past due. Ask for the money.

5. *Be businesslike*

Be businesslike in your tone. This does not mean that you should necessarily be chilly or distant, but it does mean that you should not be familiar. Your relationship with the customer has been a matter of business dealings, and a cozy friendliness may be resented.

It is also recommended that the use of humor be avoided. Debt and duns are seldom joking matters to your customer. Levity can strike the recipient as being in very bad taste.

Some humorous notices and letters have been highly effective, but there is always a chance that they will cause adverse reactions. If you do use humor, use it only in the very early phases, and make certain that the laugh is not on the debtor.

6. *Communicate*

Most important of all, be careful of your wording. If you are going to communicate with the customer, he must be able to understand your message. You must not use words which he does not have in his reading vocabulary, and you must not make your sentences too complex for him to unravel. It is difficult for persons whose work involves constant contact with written language to appreciate the difficulties other may have. Sentences which seem simple to the credit man may be only dimly understood by the customer. The meanings of words which are clear to you may be unfamiliar to your reader. Worse, he may ascribe wrong meanings to them. For example, one investigator found that most of one group he tested thought that the word "obese," meant "sinful." False notions of this kind can be disastrous to your message.

The importance of reading level is appreciated more by those who are in the field of mass communication than in other areas of business. Publishers of children's books carefully control the vocabulary. Advertising men write their copy down to an average level. A magazine which offers advice on financial affairs to the general public consciously tries to have its copy written simply and to avoid long or unfamiliar words. An expensive magazine devoted to business matters of interest more to executives is aimed at a narrower and, presumably, better educated public. This magazine makes no attempt to minimize difficulty in expression. Collection letters, certainly, should be aimed at a broader public and a high degree of literacy should not be assumed.

a. *Vocabulary.* All of the following words were found in the recommended collection letters of a good text on retail credit: arrears, jeopardize, solicit, mutual, ascertain, blemish, and accumulate. By one count, for example, "arrears" was found to occur less than two times per million words of textual matter. Although the other words given as examples occur somewhat more frequently, none was found to occur more than 18 times per million words. Satisfactory definitions of these words could be obtained from only a relatively small percentage of the population. They could all be replaced with easier words without damage to the meaning. Even words which are less obviously difficult can often be replaced with easier ones. "Thank you for your check covering a *portion* of your account," could be improved by substituting "part" for "portion." While "portion" is encountered less than 100 times in a million words, "part" is found well over 100 times and is, consequently, more likely to be known to the reader. "When you asked us recently for *an extension of time*" would be simpler if the easily understood phrase "more time," were substituted.

b. *Sentence Structure.* Reading level is affected by sentence structure as well as vocabluary. Short, simple sentences are more easily comprehended than complex or complex-compound ones. Avoid complicated expressions involving the use of clauses and long phrases. Consider this paragraph, which is just one sentence long.

"Inasmuch as it is the policy of this organization that every contact with our patrons, whether it be for the purpose of selling them merchandise or collecting for it, shall be one of considerate and courteous attention to the customer's behalf, I have withheld action on this account until I could communicate with you again and make a further effort to settle the matter in an amicable fashion."

This is not an exaggerated instance. Many sentences run on in this way, and they put a heavy burden on the reader. The same thoughts could be conveyed more easily as in the following paragraph.

"We try to make every contact with our customers a pleasant one. We want to be courteous and to consider your interests. That is why I have held up action on your account. I wanted to write you again because I am sure we can settle the matter in a friendly way."

Although there may be some quarrel with the content of the paragraph, the second form makes for easier reading. The thoughts are broken into bite-size morsels for easy chewing. The mind can pause at each period, and the reader does not have to carry so much with him as he travels from the opening to the close.

c. *Watch Your Emotional Tone.* Words and phrases which are virtually synonymous may have quite different emotional tones. The proper word should be selected to convey the emotional tone you want to get across. A familiar bit of humor illustrates this point by parsing a sentence as follows: *I* am firm, *you* are stubborn, and *he* is pig-headed. In collection correspondence you should note the distinctions between such phrases as "prompt payment" and "immediate payment." The latter phrase carries a greater sense of urgency and sounds more impatient. You can carry it one step farther with "instant payment." If you use such expressions as "a trifle overdue" or even "a small balance," you are expressing an attitude as well as a fact. A "trifle" is not worth bothering about, and, if you refer to the customer's delay in such terms, you should not be surprised if he does *not* bother about it. Likewise, if you term his debt a "small" balance, he reacts to the feeling tone as well as the fact. If $5 is a *small* balance to you and, at the moment, is is a *large* piece of money to him, he is unlikely to part with that *large* "five spot" to take care of your *small* balance.

d. *Avoid Stale Phrases.* Avoid the use of hackneyed expressions. Trite phrases like, "Permit us to state," "Awaiting your reply," "This is to advise you," or "Your esteemed patronage," detract from, rather than add to, your effect. Among the stereotyped expressions found in collection correspondence are a number which are plainly credit jargon and should also be avoided. Examples of these are, "compliance with our terms"; "unless your remittance is forthcoming"; "account is in arrears," and "unadjusted claim." It is particularly easy to allow this kind of stale phrase to creep into your sentences because it is a part of the everyday language of credit. However, there is no compelling reason why remittances must always be described as "forthcoming," or for adjustments always to be "pending." Nobody but a credit man would talk that way. Seek fresh, down-to-earth expressions which are part of the language of most people.

7. *Avoid sarcasm*

Do not succumb to the temptation to be sarcastic. People react to hostility with hostility. Not only will sarcasm alienate customers and destroy good will, but it will impede collections. Most delinquent customers feel at least a little bit guilty about their delay, and any sarcasm on your part will help them to salve their consciences. Do not give them any chance to rationalize the situation so that they can feel you are in the wrong while they are the injured parties.

8. *Motivate the customer*

Your collection letter or notice must not only ask for the money and allow the customer a way to save face, but it must also motivate him to action. The fact that you want payment is not enough; he must be impelled to pay. You must include some appeal which either (1) increases his desire to pay or (2) lowers his resistance to paying. There are a number of time-honored appeals which have been used repeatedly in the collection effort. They vary in the ingenuity with which they are phrased, but are fairly standard in their tone.

Five Standard Appeals

1. *Appeal for Cooperation.* The credit granter assumes that the credit customer has good intentions. He may gently point out how he has served the customer in the past, and ask for reciprocal courtesy.

"Have you overlooked your account with us? Your balance is now considerably past due."

"We have honestly tried to give you the very best of service and feel sure that you would want to cooperate with us by keeping your account up to date. May we have your check for the balance today?"

This appeal is also used in letters which take an individual tone. Here the phrasing is distinctly person to person.

"Will you help me?

"Frankly, I have been too free in extending credit and too much is outstanding. I must bring my accounts back into line.

"Your account is one of those past due. I would be grateful if you would give me a hand by sending your payment for the balance today."

2. *Appeal to the Desire for a Good Credit Record.* This is a very popular appeal in collection letters and notices. Although few people know much about how credit records are established, where they are maintained, or who has access to them, most people vaguely feel that it is nice to have a good one.

"Your credit rating is important. You would not want to do anything to hurt it, we are sure.

"However, the rules of the credit bureau require us to report past due accounts. We will not have to do this if you will send us your payment right away."

The variations on this theme are endless and may either be mild or severe in tone.

3. *Appeal to the Desire for Further Credit.* Although the desire for further credit is associated with the desire for a good credit record, the former is more specific. A good credit record is a somewhat nebulous thing in the minds of many, while the freedom to acquire more goods and services is concrete.

"You may need your credit at almost any time. Perhaps it will be an emergency, or maybe only a bargain you cannot afford to pass up.

"When we are called about your account with us, we want to be able to say that it is right up to date. We will be able to do this if you send payment for your balance today."

4. *Appeal to Fair Play.* This, like the appeal for cooperation, definitely assumes good faith. It mildly shames the customer for not abiding by the rules and asks him to translate his good intentions into action.

"Probably you just don't realize how long you have kept us waiting. If you wanted something from us, we would be glad to serve you promptly.

"Won't you do as much for us and send us your payment for the balance due today?"

5. *Appeal to Reputation.* This appeal has two approaches. The first flatters the customer's pride. It insinuates that a person of such fine character and high standing simply can do nothing else but pay. The second, in one degree or another, carries a threat to reputation.

"Your fine reputation among those with whom you have done business impressed us when your account was opened. We were proud to welcome you as a credit customer.

"Your balance with us is past due, however. Please justify our confidence in you by sending us a check for the balance today."

The suggestion that the customer's reputation may be damaged by continued delay in payment may either be bald or covert, subtle or obvious. The more transparent it becomes, the more likely it is to arouse hostility.

"You have had a fine repuation in our credit department, but we have been worried about your failure to reply to our notices about your account. It is considerably past due.

"A past due account is a poor credit reference when others check with us. Help us help your reputation by sending payment for your balance today."

Numerous other appeals have been mentioned in books on credit. Some of those mentioned are self-interest; satisfaction of doing the right thing; self-respect; freedom from worry; security for family; fear; being a good example to children; saving of additional expense, and job security. I am sure, however, that it has become apparent that these classifications are overlapping. They are descriptions of the thematic content of the letter or notice itself. They are concerned with what is being said to the customer rather than with the feeling or motive they are intended to arouse within him.

A Different Classification of Appeals

Avoidance

When one examines collection letters from the point of view of the recipient, the matter appears in a somewhat different light. In letters which appeal to his desire for a good credit rating, we are actually telling him that if he persists in ignoring his obligation he will have a bad credit rating. Paying his bill to you is not going to get him a good credit rating; it merely avoids adding a blemish to the record he already has whether it is currently good, bad, or indifferent. In effect, we are warning him of consequences in the hope that he will be motivated to avoid them.

When we appeal to reputation, the same thing is often true. We are suggesting that failure to meet his obligations will damage his reputation. Again, we want him to avoid this contingency. Even when we appeal to his desire for further credit, it is doubtful that we truly believe he wants something right now and will believe he has to pay us before he can get it. We are hoping that he will anticipate a future need and be fearful that he will not be able to satisfy it.

It appears then that one important group of appeals is designed to arouse avoidance of some possible unpleasant future event. The customer is supposed to feel anxious about what might happen if he does not pay.

Sense of "ought"

When we appeal to the credit customer for cooperation, we are assuming that he sees cooperativeness as a virtue. We are appealing to the "better side" of his nature, that is, the civilized side. Most people have been taught that it is "good" to cooperate with others and "bad" to take advantage of those who have treated you well. Most people have been taught that it is "nice" to give help when it is asked and "naughty" to refuse. The appeal for cooperation assumes that the customer has a background which has taught him these attitudes.

When we appeal to the sense of fair play, we are assuming that he has learned to "be a good sport" and to play by the rules. Certainly an appeal to the satisfaction of doing the right thing depends on the customer knowing what is right and caring about it.

This entire group of appeals is based on the assumption that the customer has learned the lessons of socialization, that he lives by the standards which are considered right and proper in our culture. They depend for their force on arousing a feeling of shame or guilt within him because he has not acted in the manner he has been taught is "good." On the positive side, they hope that he will be induced to seek the pleasant self-congratulatory feeling which comes from forcing one's self to perform a distasteful duty—to do what one ought to do. The first group depends primarily on avoidance while the second depends on the sense of "ought."

It is only necessary to read a metropolitan newspaper to be convinced that the sense of "ought" is not as universal as it "ought" to be. Nevertheless, the majority of people have learned to feel an internal compulsion to behave in a socialized manner and to feel disturbed when they violate the rules. Since approaches based on the sense of "ought" are less likely to arouse antagonism, are more humane, and do succeed in a large number of cases, they should be used in the initial approaches.

Principles of avoidance

When you become convinced that the customer will not be moved by his sense of "ought," you can change to the approaches based on avoidance. There are some principles which should be kept in mind when using an appeal based on avoidance.

The first of these principles is that the motivation to avoid something drops off sharply as the psychological distance from the thing which is to be avoided increases. The farther away trouble appears to be, the less it is feared. Mother may promise Junior a spanking when his father comes home, but Junior does not really begin to worry until shortly before he expects Dad. The threat of a bailiff at the door this evening produces more anxiety than the threat of a repossession next month. Many individuals have experienced the sharpness of this rise in avoidance feelings either during a visit to a dentist or before an operation. Apprehension which is mild only a few hours before the dreaded event mounts swiftly in intensity during the last few moments. It should be specifically noted that we are speaking of the *psychological* distance from the situation or event which is to be avoided. It does not matter how remote it is in reality, but only how distant it seems to be.

Of course, the lesson to be learned from this principle is that, if the appeal to avoidance is to have its greatest effect, consequences must appear to be immediate. The more distant they appear to the customer, the less is the likelihood that he will be impelled to take action on your account.

Another principle of importance is that the magnitude of the consequences is not as important as the certainty of consequences. Although the fines for speeding may be identical throughout a city, traffic moves at a more moderate pace in those areas where the laws are known to be enforced. The prospect of losing both a job and a car is only slightly more upsetting than the prospect of either loss alone. The certain prospect of unpleasant consequences is more dreaded than the possibility of total catastrophe. For example, more people worry about next week's definite problems than about atomic war. Your appeal to the credit customer will be more effective if you emphasize the idea of unavoidable and certain consequences than if you try to magnify the penalties.

How to Capture Your Customer's Attention

No matter how well you have composed your plea to the credit customer, your letter or notice will have no effect unless it captures the customer's attention. If he does not attend to the notice, no matter how good the appeal may be, there will be no collection. This is particularly important because your letter is competing with a flow of other mail, advertisements which seek to sell him more and, probably, notices from other creditors. Anything which can be done to give your letter an advantage from the standpoint of getting attention is important.

There are certain characteristics of things which usually command attention. For example, loud, bright, moving, or unusual things tend to be noticed. So do things which appeal to an individual's interests.

Size

Size is certainly one characteristic which affects the attention things receive. Large things get more attention than small ones. People tend to remember the contents of letters on larger stationery better than they do those on smaller sizes. Making collection letters and notices of larger size is one way to increase the attention they receive.

Repetition

Another way to command attention is through repetition. The sound from the splash of one drop of water may go unnoticed, but the incessant dripping of a leaky faucet can rivet attention to itself and defy efforts to ignore it. The same can be true of the ticking of a clock. Perhaps the dripping of the faucet is somewhat more compelling than the ticking of the clock because of the little variations in the sound. It is not so easy for the dripping to become part of the expected and habitual background of little noises. Similarly, repeated notices or letters each with a little variation in size, format, or content will gain attention where a single notice would not. One large notice or letter, followed by a smaller version of the same thing, with yet another in which the format is changed will likely be attended to.

It should be noted that if there is too much time lag between repeated notices, the effect is lost. A series of notices mailed on the same day each week will definitely produce an effect which cannot be duplicated with any single notice. Shorter periods do not allow enough time for mail to be returned or for the debtor to respond. Also, if shorter regular intervals are selected, the mailing date will occasionally fall on a Sunday.

Motion

Motion attracts attention. This is why it is used in electric signs and window displays. While real motion may not be incorporated into a collection notice, suggested motion may. A finger stabbing at a book titled "Credit Record" appropriately streaked to indicate movement may arouse interest. The use of illustrations in your notices can enable you to employ this attention getting element.

Isolation

An object standing by itself commands attention. This is why smart advertisers fight the temptation to put too much on a page. The expanse of white space helps the message draw attention. Likewise, the collection man should design his notices so that they are not cluttered, so that the text is suitably isolated. This method of gaining attention lends itself well to novelty notices—perhaps a large asterisk in the center of the page with the collection message at the bottom.

Novelty

Novelty also commands attention and may be incorporated in your notices and letters by clever phraseology, exaggeration of some aspect, unusual typography, size, shape, or illustration. You should be careful, however, that you do not subordinate your purpose to being clever. A notice may be novel enough to command attention and still fail to get its message across. As previously noted, some people do not feel that debts and duns are anything to joke about.

Color

Color is related to attention. Those colors toward the red end of the spectrum seem to have a slightly higher attention getting value than those toward the blue end. The use of color has been shown to have definite advantages in direct mail selling and in advertising. There is good reason to believe it also improves the effectiveness of collection letters and notices. If colored paper or inks are to be used, there should be sufficient contrast between type and background to insure easy readability.

Legibility

In designing collection notices, you should give attention to the legibility of your typography. The most legible type faces have fairly heavy strokes throughout. Combining light and heavy strokes reduces legibility. Italics, script, or Old English are less legible than the ordinary Roman type face.

It does not follow, though, that your notice would be most legible if you did the whole thing in capitals, because most people do not read words letter by letter. They recognize them rather by the general pattern and shape much as they recognize the face of a friend. A few words set in upper case would be satisfactory, but the majority of your appeal should be set in lower case.

You should not try to incorporate all of these devices in any one mailing piece. It is necessary only that your letter or notice command enough attention and hold it long enough for your message to be read.

Differences Between Notices and Letters

Up to this point, letters and notices have been discussed together, because many of the principles relating to their use and structure are the same. There are, however, differences between letters and notices which should be considered.

A letter, even if it is not individually typed, is more of a person-to-person communication than is the notice. The letter is typically signed, and the content is what one individual is saying to another. Even though he may be acting officially rather than personally, he is still talking in the first person. A printed notice is not as personal as the letter. It is more likely to be regarded as coming from the "company" than from a person within the company. The customer is likely to respond to the letter with, "I got a letter from you this morning," but to the notice, "Your outfit sent me a notice yesterday." Perhaps it is for this reason that notices are more commonly used in the early stages of the collection effort.

However, the use of notices does not have to be confined to the first stages. Although impersonality should be the keynote of the first efforts at collection, it is not necessarily out of place in the later phases. Notices can be designed to carry increasing degrees of urgency. They can, in fact, be prepared to suit almost any purpose in the collection campaign.

The notice is different from the letter also in that a letter demands a special style of format. If you depart too much from the conventional pattern, the letter ceases to be perceived as a letter. The style and form of a letter place certain restrictions on what can be said and how you can say it. You are more or less forced to use the first person to second person form of address. It is not as easy to use indirect suggestion or implication when you are so confined.

One of the notices used by National Accounts System (Figure 1) illustrates the use of indirect suggestion in a notice. You will note that there is no mention of legal action of any kind in the words on the notice. The only source for such an idea is in the drawing on the notice. The arm with its judicial robe and gavel implies the possibility of suit. This implication is not missed by those who receive the notice. National Accounts System receives numerous calls about this notice. Many people state that they received a notice threatening suit. This is the primary impression they have gained. Since the notice is employed only for accounts too small to justify legal action, an open threat of suit would be inappropriate. The implication, however, is enough to get action from many who have failed to react to previous notices.

Figure 1

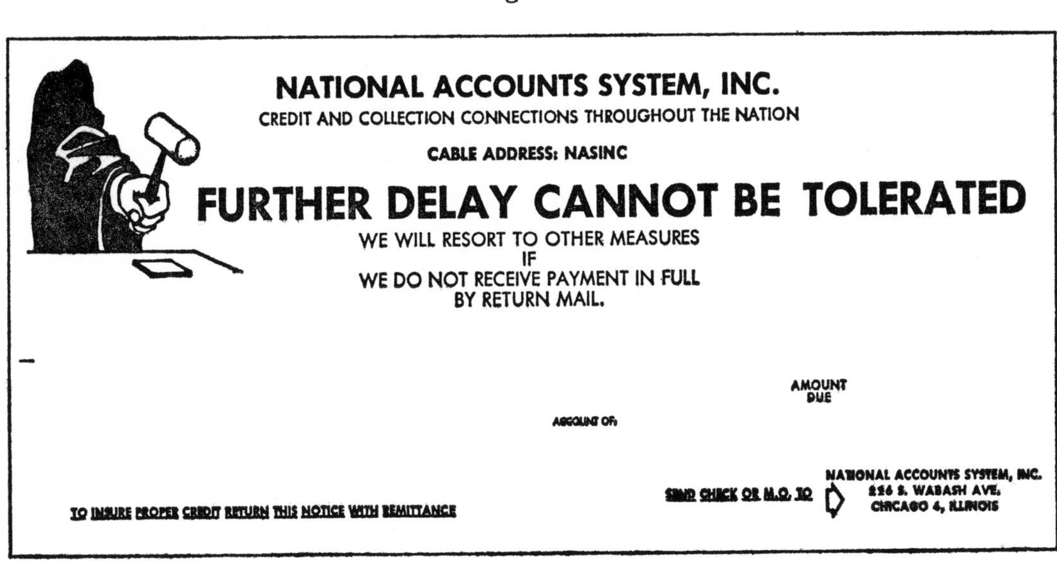

NATIONAL ACCOUNTS SYSTEM, INC.
CREDIT AND COLLECTION CONNECTIONS THROUGHOUT THE NATION
CABLE ADDRESS: NASINC

FURTHER DELAY CANNOT BE TOLERATED

WE WILL RESORT TO OTHER MEASURES
IF
WE DO NOT RECEIVE PAYMENT IN FULL
BY RETURN MAIL.

AMOUNT DUE

ACCOUNT OF:

TO INSURE PROPER CREDIT RETURN THIS NOTICE WITH REMITTANCE

SEND CHECK OR M.O. TO NATIONAL ACCOUNTS SYSTEM, INC.
226 S. WABASH AVE.
CHICAGO 4, ILLINOIS

Collection notice illustrating the use of indirect suggestion.

The conventional style of a letter also limits the extent to which some of the attention getting devices previously discussed may be employed. The notice gives a much wider latitude for unusual layout, striking use of color, and illustrations. Bold type, odd shapes and sizes of paper stock, and effective use of white space can be more easily incorporated into the design of a notice.

There is more temptation to be wordy in a letter than in a notice. Both the writer and the recipient may feel that a very brief letter is abrupt, even though the letter may be very courteously worded. The letter writer tends to add paragraphs after the subject is already adequately covered. Brevity in the printed notice is more easily accomplished and more easily accepted by the reader.

Letters, too, have their advantages. The more personal flavor of the letter can be desirable. If you are offering to help the debtor find a way out of his difficulties, the offer will be received with better grace if it is in letter form. If you want to make an appeal for cooperation or fair play on a person-to-person basis, the letter style is necessary. If you want the debtor to feel singled out for individual attention, a printed notice is not suitable.

Nevertheless, when all the advantages of the notice are considered one wonders why notices are not more widely used. It does not seem that their potential has been fully exploited.

Since form letters and notices are the most widely used collection tools, studied care should go into their construction. While the design and phrasing of the best forms is a matter more of ingenuity than mechanics, errors can be avoided by observing certain principles. The phrasing of the appeal should be clear, the appeal itself should be appropriate—and your message should command attention.

GENERAL PRINCIPLES OF COLLECTION BY TELEPHONE

X

GENERAL PRINCIPLES OF COLLECTION BY TELEPHONE

Usually the customer is not called on the telephone until several pieces of mail have been sent without a response. The telephone call, as a collection procedure, is not generally employed until the account has become considerably delinquent. The creditor hesitates to make the matter so personal an issue. Up to a point, this hesitation is sensible. Many persons would greatly resent receiving a telephone call about a debt which was only a little past due. However, there is a tendency to hesitate too long and to rely on letters and notices past the point when it should be clear that they will not produce results. As a consequence, the personal telephone call becomes one of the desperation measures.

Telephone Calls Detect Grievances

The tendency to postpone calling the customer should be resisted. The telephone call is not only a better collection tool, but it is also often preferable from the viewpoint of customer relations. It is possible that the customer's refusal to respond to your mail stems from some grievance. The personal telephone call is the best device for detecting such complaints. Adjustments may often be quickly arranged in the give and take of a telephone conversation.

There is no reason why some prescribed ritual must be completed before the customer is telephoned. Many finance companies dispense with notices after an account is three weeks delinquent, feeling that it is best to telephone sooner so that the problem can be known. Neither fear of antagonizing the customer, nor reluctance to becoming involved in a delicate interpersonal situation should deter you from calling when it is appropriate. If you use tact in your contacts, you fears will be unfounded, and it is usually appropriate to call sooner than is customary. Any time in the collection sequence that it becomes apparent to the collector the customer will not respond to mail appeals, it is appropriate to telephone him.

Six Distinctive Features of Telephone Communication

If telephone calls to the customer are to be most effective, some features of this kind of communication should be kept in mind. Talking to someone on the telephone is quite different from letter writing or face-to-face conversation. Some of the distinctive features of telephone conversation are merely converses of those features of communication by letter which were discussed earlier, while others are peculiar to the telephone situation.

1. *Demands attention*

When you make a telephone call, there is little problem of gaining attention. The telephone commands attention. While it is easy completely to ignore a letter one does not want to open, few people have the stamina to resist answering the phone. If the customer is there, the insistent and compelling ringing of his phone will insure that you have a chance to get your message to him.

2. *Interrupts*

The telephone call interrupts other activity. Whatever the customer is doing when your call is made will be put aside in favor of talking with you. The familiar, and presumably, humorous situation of receiving a telephone call while in the bath is only one of many inconvenient circumstances which can attend your call to the customer. Further, unless the customer tells you, there is little chance that you will know in just what circumstances you did catch him. This unknown factor in the situation can seriously affect the tone and the outcome of your conversation. It is, of course, wise to do whatever you can to find out if your call finds him in circumstances favorable to your purpose.

Sometimes, after identifying yourself, it is well to ask, "Is it convenient for you to talk with me now?" This practice makes it less likely that your efforts will be defeated solely because of an unfortunate accident of timing. Since it is always inconvenient for some credit customers to talk about their bills, you should take precautions when you are told that your call comes at an inconvenient time. For this reason you should ask, "When will it be convenient?" Try to obtain some specific time at a specific telephone number when you can discuss your business. Failing in this, you may accept the customer's promise to call you, but, again, the time he is to call must be made definite.

Attention to the convenience of the customer is appropriate more in earlier collection efforts. In later efforts a willingness to defer the conversation until later conveys a lack of urgency and gives the customer additional time to devise his strategy. In fact, in later collection efforts, it may be to your advantage to catch him at inconvenient times.

3. *Voice alone must do the job*

Both parties to a telephone conversation are stripped of all personal characteristics other than voice. Neither person has the advantage of facial expression or gesture to help him to communicate or to assist him in interpreting the meaning of the other person. As a result, the timbre of your voice, the pacing of your words, the intonation you use, and the emphasis you place all have greater importance. Your voice and the way you use it must carry the whole burden of communicating your personality. Whether you intend it or not, the person at the other end of the line is forming an image of you which fits the voice he hears. Similarly, you are forming an image in your mind of the other person. Each of you is reacting to this image in his behavior to the other.

4. *Requires immediate response*

Remarks made to one another by telephone—like a face-to-face conversation, but unlike a letter—require a more or less instant response from the other party. There is little time for reflection, and these responses are more likely to be spontaneous. This is both an advantage and a disadvantage for the collector. It allows him more of an opportunity to evaluate the customer's real motives and meanings, but it also puts pressure on him to make the best moves to accomplish his purpose quickly. The customer may tell you things he would have concealed if he had had time to deliberate. He may be less adept in his efforts to dissemble, and he may falter in his defenses. But the collector is equally challenged. He must be alert to all that is said and implied by the customer and, at the same time, select the best response from a host of alternatives. He must be both a participant in the conversation and an observer of it. He must be simultaneously involved and detached.

5. *Easily ended*

A telephone conversation may be terminated easily and at will. If the situation becomes too unpleasant or if the customer begins to feel that he is losing ground, he can hang up. It is much easier to do this than to walk away from a personal conversation. This option is an advantage for your respondent and is one which many customers exercise.

Although collectors are well aware that the customer may hang up, not all of them know that they, too, can end the conversation at a point convenient for their purposes. This can be done very tactfully by breaking the connection while you are yourself talking. When you do this, you leave the impression that you were cut off. Few people would believe that you would deliberately interrupt your own remarks.

6. *Person to person relation*

The telephone call involves a relationship between two persons. Whether you are acting as an agent for your company or not, you are perceived by the customer as an individual. A specific person is calling him, not a company. All of the traditions and customs which relate to interpersonal and social situations are involved. Special forms and courtesies must be observed. Both you and the customer are cast in certain roles. You must behave in a certain way because of your function in the situation—because of what you are doing. Likewise, the customer is cast in his role. He, too, has a limited choice of behavior because of his position. The problem of status enters into the relationship. The situation demands that one of you have a dominant position. Who gets that position is of critical importance. You want it, because your goal is to influence the behavior of the customer—in a sense, to control him.

In all your conversations with delinquent customers, everything you say and do should exude confidence in the result. You should never allow your words, or your manner, to reflect the slightest uncertainty about the eventual outcome. The customer should get the impression that you could never entertain any doubt that he will pay.

Words for Control

There are basically only two ways to influence and control the behavior of other persons. You can control others through physical force or through the use of symbols. Since the avenue of physical force is obviously closed to you, the only approach is through the use of symbols, chiefly words. In order for these symbols to be effective it is necessary that they be understood by the person whom you are seeking to influence. Obviously, your pleas for payment will not be successful if you are talking with someone who does not understand English.

What do you mean?

It is not so obvious, however, that you can both be speaking English and still not understand one another because of the differences in the meanings you each attach to words. "Cooperation," for example, means many things to many people. Everyone believes that he "cooperates," but everyone also knows that people "cooperate" quite differently. Other words and phrases may have similar variations in their meanings. What is "fair play" to one person may be a "dirty trick" to another. Certainly all people do not see the same things as being "obligations." The more abstract your words become, the greater becomes your risk of creating misunderstanding. You will encounter least difficulty in communicating about very concrete concepts like "money," "payment," and "Friday."

The meanings of the symbols we, as members of our society, use to communicate with one another, the words and gestures of everyday life, must be learned by each new member. This is a part of the socialization process already mentioned. Each person must, and usually does, learn as he grows to maturity just what behavior is right and acceptable and what behavior is wrong and unacceptable. Your effect in any collection effort, and particularly on the telephone, hinges on the success of this early training in forming the conscience of the customer. If your appeals to socialized motives are to be effective at all, they must strike some responsive chord in the customer's moral ideas, attitudes or values.

Evoking Effective Emotions

Only to the extent that the customer has learned to feel guilt or shame for evading debt can any appeal evoke these feelings in him. Guilt is actually punishment which one inflicts on himself for breaking the rules of an internalized code. One feels guilty when his conscience is bothering him, and his conscience only bothers him when he has done something he has learned is wrong. Shame is felt when one's bad conduct becomes known to others and causes him to lose face. One can feel shame only to the extent that he has learned to care about the opinions of those with whom he has lost face. If the groups which are important to him see nothing to be ashamed of in evading debt, he will not feel shame. It is quite possible to feel shame for actions for which one does not feel guilt.

If your appeals to avoidance behavior are to be effective, the customer must have learned to fear the dangers you would have him anticipate. There are a few things which most people fear such as physical pain, death, and the ridicule or scorn of associates, but even these are feared by different persons in different degrees. The same things are not feared by all persons. One learns what to fear and how fearful these things are. The serious scientist may fear publicity while the politician may seek it. More to the point, loss of credit standing may be highly dangerous to a businessman, but of little importance to an itinerant farm laborer. The threat of legal action may lack motivating force because of ignorance concerning the possible consequences of suit or because of fortunate experiences with it in the past.

Recognize the Customer's Feelings

If a collector or credit man comes from the typical middle class background, he will have fairly definite feelings about financial obligations. His parents and playmates will have trained him to honor his promises. Quite probably he may have had one or more rather painful experiences as a result of violating some of the standards of financial conduct which his family considered right and proper. By the time he is an adult, however, he no longer needs the presence of parents or police to keep him from infractions of this code. Honest financial behavior is so much a part of his standards for himself that any other course of action just would not seem natural. If he let a debt drag on for months, he would feel guilty. If his friends found out that he was being dunned, he would feel ashamed. He would feel anxious if he thought that an adverse report might be made to the credit bureau.

These standards and attitudes may seem so natural to him that he finds it difficult to understand how some people can feel quite different. If he is to be a good telephone collector, however, it is necessary that he learn to understand individuals who do come from different backgrounds and have, quite "naturally," different attitudes. He must learn to detect these differences in the persons with whom he talks and to infer from little bits of evidence the general pattern of their standards. Then he must learn to talk their language.

Talking the Customer's Language

Learning to "talk the language" of persons from a different background than one's own involves more than learning the words of their particular jargon. It involves talking about meaningful topics, discussing these topics in terms which are important to that individual, and putting the discussion at a level which is understandable to the other person. The unskilled laborer, for example, is much less likely to be concerned about the possibility that you may "consult with his employer" than about the notion that you "might talk with his boss." Reference to integrity may motivate one person, but be incomprehensible to another.

Talking the language of the other person requires a sensitivity to the values which are important to him. Among some groups there is a premium put on toughness, there is a reliance on luck, and status may be gained from the ability to deceive or to take advantage of others. Among different groups decidedly opposite values prevail. An approach which would be effective with the more gently bred might get nothing but contempt from some of these less privileged persons. If you want to get your meaning understood, you should not talk to a stevedore in the same terms you would use with a bookkeeper.

Among certain elements in our country there is a growing feeling that the ultimate responsibility for the welfare of each individual lies with the state or some other social structure. Their behavior seems to reveal the belief that personal responsibility ends with the effort to provide for themselves on a day-to-day basis. If some unexpected event interferes with their daily income, they appear to feel that this excuses them from current obligations. Every collector has heard credit customers tell him that a strike is on, not as an apology or an excuse, but in the full belief and expectation that the strike makes non-payment legitimate, that it absolves them of any current obligation to pay. Among such groups, credit is coming to be regarded more as a right than as a privilege. Credit is seen as an obligation the creditor owes to the buyer. These attitudes, too, the collector must be able to detect and to understand.

Recognize the Customer as an Individual

In collecting by mail, you have to appeal to the generalized customer. You select and phrase your appeal so that it will motivate a majority. In telephone collecting, on the other hand, you are not dealing with the average person or the typical person: you are always dealing with an individual. You must be responsive to individual differences. Persons differ not only in attitudes, but in intelligence, education, age, income, and in numerous other ways. If you find that your customer is somewhat dull, you should adjust your vocabulary so that you do not talk over his head. Further, you should make your remarks in a more deliberate manner in order to give him time to absorb one idea before you go to another. With such customers you will find it to your advantage to repeat yourself several times, perhaps even using the same words. It is sometimes advisable to ask him to get pencil and paper and write down certain critical items such as the amount and the address to which the payment should be sent.

Your approach to the person in a higher income bracket who is living beyond his means will be somewhat different than to the one who is earning only a bare subsistence. In the first case your goal is to divert from other channels to your direction some of the money which is already being spent. You want to establish the priority of your claim on his funds. In the second case, you may find yourself engaged in helping the person budget himself or obtain a loan. You will note that the difference in approach is not determined by a moral judgment concerning the character or worth of two persons, but on a rational decision about the best approach to the problem of obtaining payment.

Learn to Listen

It is essential to remember that each contact with a customer is different, and, while some general principles can be stated, your approach to each person should be largely tailored for that particular individual. This, of course, means that you should be familiar with all the information available on the credit application and ledger card before you make the call. It further means that you should listen carefully to the customer so that you pick up every clue he gives you about himself. You should not only listen to what he says but also be alert to what he does not say. When the context of a conversation seems to demand something which is not said, this fact should be noted. We are all accustomed to sudden shifts in conversation, to persons going ahead with their train of thought, and to comments which do not seem to follow what went before. In collecting, however, you should notice these shifts. They are not accidental. Consider the following fragment from a collection call.

Collector: But you are working now, Mr. Jones?
Customer: I told you I'll get the money to you just as soon as I can.

The customer's failure to react to the collector's question is probably significant. One cannot infer too much from such a short sample of conversation, but it does seem probable that the customer does not want to answer the question. He was trying to steer the collector away from that area of inquiry by giving him something else of value; that is, a promise to pay. One would suspect his sincerity. Perhaps another example will help to clarify this point.

Collector: You say your husband has been in the hospital, Mrs. Jones.
Mrs. Jones: Uh-huh.
Collector: How long do you expect him to be hospitalized?
Mrs. Jones: I don't know.
Collector: Didn't the doctor give you any idea?
Mrs. Jones: No. He didn't say.

In this case it is possible that the collector is dealing with a person who is merely dull, but this fact would have to be verified by reference to the rest of the conversation. If it is not a case of dullness, one has good cause to suspect dishonesty. The truly sincere customer would be likely to volunteer such items as the name of the hospital, the nature of the illness, and whether it appeared that the stay would be long or short. He is truly in trouble and wants you to believe him. He documents his story to make it convincing.

Sometimes the customer says too much. He over-elaborates his story with details, many of which cannot be verified. This, too, should be noted. You should not only observe what he says to you, but wonder about why he said it. Do not pass up slips of the tongue as sheer accidents. Often things slip out that the person with whom you are talking did not mean to tell you. This may happen, for example, on names. If the debtor says, "Rufus. No, I mean Roscoe," you may well ask who Rufus is. Remember your chances of collecting may well depend on what you know about this person. Learn all you can.

Get Customer Facts

You should always be conscious of the fact that you may need leverage, and leverage is often provided by information about the customer, particularly in the areas of assets and income. Always try to find out, if you do not already know, where the customer is employed. It will also be useful to know his wife's employment if you can get this. Knowing whether he owns a car may be useful. Pick up information of this kind as you talk with the customer about payment.

In getting information, it is frequently a good tactic to make an assumption and put the burden of denying it on the other person. For example, in attempting to find out if the customer has a car, you might ask, "What kind of car do you drive?" If the customer owns a car and it appears that you already know this, there is little motivation to hide the fact. You can follow this up with, "How much are your payments?" and "Where do you make your payments?" The automobile finance companies often keep track of their customers when other creditors fail.

In attempting to discover from his wife the employment of a husband, you might assume a job, e.g., "Your husband is the Richard Roe who is a capper for the ABC Bottling Company, isn't he?" Perhaps this maneuver stands even more of a chance for success if the job you assume is known to be a low status job. Often these questions elicit vigorous denials documented by the real occupation and employer. Your strategy will work best if it is not too far-fetched. It stands the best chance of success if it looks like it could be an honest error on your part.

This same procedure can also be used with the customer himself, but it requires just a little more histrionic ability. The conversation might go something like this. "Is this Richard Q. Roe?" "Yeah." "You are the Richard Roe who is the grape presser for the ABC Wine Co., aren't you?" "No, I drive a cab for Spotless." "Well, your address is 333 Baker Place, isn't it?" "Yep." "And your telephone number is Park 1-1111?" "Sure is." "Then, you're the right one. I don't know how I got mixed up on the other."

Four Chief Customer's Defenses

You begin to find out about the customer as a unique person when you make your first call to him. At this time he ceases to be a collection of facts on paper and begins to take on body and substance. In your initial call you should give him an opportunity to reveal himself. The best procedure for opening the conversation is to identify yourself, your company, state that you are calling about his account, and mention the balance. Then, you wait. Do not plunge ahead into arguments or persuasion. Do not recite your attempts to collect by mail. Merely let the matter hang and be in no hurry to fill up the conversational vacuum. The customer's reaction to this situation can tell you a great deal about how you will have to approach the matter.

1. *Aggression and attack*

Look at it from his point of view. Although the customer may be well aware of the debt and may even have been expecting a call eventually, he did not know that it was coming at this time. He is not completely prepared. His reaction is quite likely to be characteristic of his behavior in other kinds of emergency situations. Suppose he begins to complain about the goods or services. It may well be that he typically defends himself against threats by attacking. If you, in turn, attack, he will become increasingly aggressive. This could lead to a highly charged and angry session from which the customer can draw more support for the position that he is being treated badly. This will certainly not improve your chances for collecting. Perhaps your first impulse is to challenge his contention. If he had a complaint to make, why did he not make it before? He had plenty of time before you called him.

It is usually best to resist this impulse and not to challenge him. He can find plenty of excuses for his behavior and you would be off on the wrong foot and in the wrong direction. Your best tactic is to express your pleasure at the fact that you have now found out the cause of the delay, and tell him how willing you will be to adjust any complaints he may have. If this cannot be done over the telephone, make a specific appointment to see him in person. Get him to commit himself to a certain time at which he will come in. If his complaint is a legitimate one, you will have made a friend for your company. If it was merely a stall, you have made it difficult for him to continue his defense. It is hard to fight with someone who meets belligerence with cooperation and pleasantness.

2. *Begging for sympathy*

Suppose the customer acknowledges the debt and begins a recital of his financial and personal woes. Again, it may be the unvarnished truth or it may be that this person habitually defends himself by playing on the sympathies of others. In either case it is not wise to argue with his story. The past cannot be remedied. You are seeking payment now or in the near future. Express sympathy for the customer's difficulties, but be persistent in your insistence that the debt must be paid. If the customer is in trouble, both humanity and good business practice dictate that you should make arrangements for an extension. You certainly should not treat the matter casually, however. The customer should not get the impression that such arrangements are made routinely. Make the matter a serious one, preferably conducted at your office through a personal interview. Make the terms specific and impress them on the customer. The solemnity and gravity with which you make such arrangements is even more important when the plea of sympathy is not true or only half true. If such customers find that it is easy to arrange extensions, they are apt to find themselves in numerous future emergencies.

3. *Denial and evasion*

The customer may react to your telephone call by denying that he has received any statements or notices at all. You should, of course, verify his identity and address. If corrections in the address are needed, you should make them. But, if the address is correct, you may be tempted to challenge his truthfulness. Again, resist the impulse. There is no profit in establishing the fact that he is lying, even if he is. You should, rather, review the account with him, establish the existence of the debt, and request immediate payment. It is particularly desirable to get a clear admission of the debt because it narrows the range of excuses he can offer. An admission of the debt leaves open only the question of when payment will be made.

Since the customer has given you a hint about his chief mode of defense by his initial reaction—that is, untruth and evasion—you can expect more of the same. He may promise payment and then fail to keep his promise. Prompt follow-up on this promise may meet with another stall. He may say he sent payment to you and that it must have been lost in the mail.

He may say he forgot and give you another promise. He may give you almost any conceivable excuse for his failure. You should remember, though, that behind these excuses lies a cause which the excuses are intended to conceal. If he has admitted the debt, it is most likely that he is short of funds or overburdened with debt. If you can get the customer into your office, you stand the best chance of finding out the truth and making realistic arrangements for payment.

4. *Defiance*

Another customer may simply say, "So what?" This reaction is the one which is most likely to leave the inexperienced collector dumbfounded. It is so contrary to the ordinary and expected attitude that he may have no response available to counter it other than to gulp and to stammer. It is very important, though, in dealing with this response, that the collector maintain his composure and his command of the situation. He should remain cool and polite. His answer should be a direct request for payment of the account.

The "so what" response is clearly antagonistic and is one calculated to provoke an argument. You would do best to decline the bid. In the first place, argument will scarcely ever succeed with an individual like this. Secondly, your refusal to become aroused may lead him to continue to press his attack. In so doing he may reveal the true motives for his behavior and thus give you an opportunity to reach a constructive solution.

If, on the other hand, the customer blandly says he is not going to pay and refuses to give reasons, it is probably best to tell him that it will be placed for collection on a certain date. Make the date soon, and, if payment is not made by that date, carry out your promise and place the account for collection.

These are only a few of the major responses in an infinite variety of reactions to a collection call. The important thing to note from these examples is that the customer feels himself in a position where he must defend himself. Your call may be seen as a threat to his self-esteem, and his excuses may be offered merely to redeem himself in your eyes. Your call may be felt as a danger to his financial security, and he is seeking safety. People have more or less favorite ways of meeting such threats. Some tend to run away from troubles. This they can do by physically moving, lying, or postponing. Some stand up to troubles and slug it out. This they can do by fighting, arguing, and sarcasm. Some try to talk themselves into believing that it is not their fault. This they can do by blaming someone else, distorting their memory of what actually happened, or even by forgetting. Some, fortunately, try to find solutions and take constructive action. These modes of defense tend to be characteristic for each individual. You learn something about this typical behavior in the customer's reaction to your initial call. You get a clue to the way in which he handles his problems.

Let Your Brain Control the Conversation

Your responses to the customer and your remarks to him should be based on an intelligent and reasoned appraisal of the problem he presents. When you select an action, you should be making a logical choice, not just reacting in a conventional or social way. You are engaging in a conversation with a purpose, and that purpose is neither to vent your feelings nor to socialize. You may be tempted, when your conversation has been a pleasant one, to prolong the matter and to chat. Such conversations should not be drawn out merely because they are enjoyable. You should terminate them just as soon as you can do so and still leave a good impression.

On the other hand, you will be met with hostility in many of your contacts with delinquent customers. It is natural to react to hostility with hostility. If you allow yourself to take the hostility personally and to react with anger, you will not only find yourself under an unnecessary and unpleasant strain, but you will also be less effective in collecting. Anger and strong emotions get in the way of the higher intellectual functions. Try to remember that the customer is venting his hostility on you as a symbol rather than as a person. He is angry at the situation, he resents being disciplined, or he is just mad at the world.

You will find that on some occasions merely absorbing the customer's anger impassively produces surprising results. Some customers, after getting the poison out of their systems, actually come through with payment. Others, when they fail to arouse anger in you, have no defense left. They just do not know how to cope with people if they cannot make them angry.

The collector should view the situation as he would other intellectual problems. He should be thinking about the customer more than he should be feeling about him. His approach should be dispassionate and logical rather than social or emotional. While the physician may feel sympathy for the pain and distress of his patients, he must not allow his emotional reactions to interfere with a rational approach to treatment. Neither should the collector allow emotions to interfere with his efforts to find a constructive way to accomplish his purpose.

The collector should remember that, in a real sense, he is acting as an agent of society. He is trying to insure that individuals honor their contracts. Contracts are among the basic institutions which society has evolved to make possible an ordered and predictable relationship among its members. Violations of contract are threats to this ordered relationship and, if permitted to flourish, would shake the very foundations of our society.

This certainly does not mean that the collector should be heartless or callous in his relationships with customers. Law, custom, and considerations of humanity insist that relief be given to those too heavily burdened. Few businessmen would care to pursue the collection of accounts to the point where their efforts would cause true misery or suffering to others. In their sympathy for the individual, however, businessmen must remember their responsibility to a larger group, the owners of the business, the employees, and the other customers. They must not allow the few to exploit the many. While relief must be accorded the victims of hardship, care should be exercised to prevent the unworthy from taking advantage of this kind of leniency. Business firms may contribute to charitable and philanthropic organizations, but they cannot function as charities and remain in business. Sympathy, untempered by thought and judgment, can lead to actions which encourage the spendthrift and the ne'er-do-well, teach lack of foresight and planning to the already thoughtless, and result in disaster to a business enterprise. The collector must remain objective as he evaluates collection problems.

How to Cultivate a Collection Personality

An intelligent and objective approach, by itself, is not enough. You must also present the kind of personality to the customer to which the customer will react favorably. Personality, as it is used here, refers to the impact you have when you are talking to him on the telephone. It has little to do with the way your wife sees you, the way you see yourself, or the way you behave at a party. As used here, it is what you sound like on the telephone. It is the image which is formed at the other end of the line. You convey this personality to the customer in the timbre and pitch of your voice, your choice of words, your inflection, the pacing of your remarks, and in the attitude you take. Your telephone personality should have a variety of aspects just as does your personality in other situations.

It is possible to point out certain general characteristics of an effective telephone personality for collection purposes. These *general* characteristics are only *generally* effective, however. At home you may be cordial under some circumstances, you may become stern if the children misbehave, or you may be jovial with close friends. Your collection personality should also have many facets. You should be flexible in your approach so that you can present these different facets as the occasion calls for them.

1. *Sound confident*

Speaking generally, the collector should sound confident and mature. His voice should communicate a feeling of authority. He should sound like the kind of person whom people respect.

2. *Sound businesslike*

Although the collector's tone should be businesslike, it should not be brusque. The tone should be natural and carry the ring of sincerity. The customer should be able to feel that there is a real person behind the words he hears. A businesslike tone does not mean one which is rigidly aloof and studiously impersonal. It does not mean that you should cultivate an artificial or machine-like style.

A businesslike tone is one which treats serious matters seriously, and states facts with conviction and assurance. A businesslike tone is set when positive and complete sentences are spoken without hesitation or stammer. The businesslike tone can be friendly, but not familiar. A certain degree of social distance is advisable and appropriate in business dealings. Flip attitudes and expressions such as "all rightey" or "okey dokey" just do not fit. Firmness is even more convincing when it is coupled with formal courtesy.

3. *Be courteous*

Of course you should be courteous. There is no need for rudeness and nothing to be gained from it. You should conduct yourself with dignity and decorum. If the person to whom you are talking resorts to gutter tactics and talk, there is certainly no reason for you to follow him down. You can be firm without being vulgar, or indignant without being coarse.

4. *Be flexible*

There will most certainly be occasions on which you will wish to modify the image you convey. Perhaps you will find a defiant customer who may yield to a firmer tone, and you feel it advisable to put a slight chill in the air. You should be able to do so without becoming either nasty or unpleasant. On the other hand, you may feel that another person may yield to a sympathetic and understanding tone. You should be able to turn on more warmth without becoming too personal. Perhaps, even, there will be a rare occasion on which you will want to put your appeal in terms of a personal favor to you and decide to become a little chummy. Consider this course carefully first, because it invites the customer, in turn, to become chummy with you. You can find yourself at a serious disadvantage if the personal appeal does not work.

In collection by telephone, you will inevitably talk to persons other than customers. For example, children may answer the phone. They can be quite important and helpful to you. You, of course, should be warm and winning and take care to avoid giving offense. A boy can be quite annoyed if you should say, "Are you her daughter?" This is an easy mistake when you are trying to judge sex from the telephone voice of children, and girls can be just as offended as boys when you err. One way to avoid this embarrassment is to give your name and ask that of the child. In most cases you will get more cooperation from children if you avoid talking down to them. Treat the child with respect and courtesy. Thank him as you would an adult. Young girls are particularly flattered to be addressed as "Miss."

You will also probably find yourself talking with employers, personnel managers, and foremen. Your attitude should be one which acknowledges that you are asking a favor and one which invites cooperation from them. You should be respectful, courteous, grateful for any help you receive, and, above all, sincere. You can be all these things without demeaning yourself.

You may find the telephone at the customer's address answered by a hostile and uncooperative custodian or janitor. Even though his main answer may be "no," you can get cooperation and help from him if you can adjust your attitude quickly. Softening him up may require both tact and ingenuity, but it can be done if you are flexible enough.

5. *Be natural*

In most situations, the collector should try to use good grammar and a simple vocabulary. He should avoid both slang and stilted phrases. His speech should be natural. He should strive for simple and uncomplicated sentences. His delivery should be unhurried and deliberate. Firecracker styles are hard to understand and require repetition. You will save time if you give your words time to soak in. Do not rush to get it all said before you take a breath.

All of this adds up to the fact that the best telephone collector is one who can change roles quickly. He can present the personality needed to get results. He is a diplomat, a salesman, and an actor. He is aware of the advantages and the limitations of the telephone. He is alert to the nuances of conversation and adapts himself to the differences in individuals. He is in control of himself and his emotions.

SOME SPECIFICS OF TELEPHONE COLLECTION

XI

SOME SPECIFICS OF TELEPHONE COLLECTION

In collection by telephone there will be a number of recurrent situations for which it is possible to develop fairly specific techniques. There are a number of errors which can be avoided if they are pointed out in advance. While it is not possible to anticipate these for all credit granters, it is possible to give some fairly definite rules for collecting in most situations. By observing these rules the collector can, at least, reduce his errors in dealing with people by telephone.

Thirteen Telephone Collection Musts

1. *Check identity of your party*

One important rule for telephone collection is, know to whom you are talking. You may assume that your mail reaches the person to whom it is addressed, but you should not assume that the person who answers the telephone is the one you thought you were calling. You may have dialed a wrong number, you may have reached the wrong person at the right number, or the telephone number may have been re-assigned. Be specific in establishing the identity of the other person. The last name alone is not enough identification. The opening of a collection call could go somewhat as follows:

Collector: Hello. May I speak with Mrs. Doe, please?
Voice: This is Mrs. Doe.
Collector: Mrs. Doe, this is Mr. Roe of the XYZ Company. I am calling about your balance of $53.49.
Voice: What balance?

Collector: Why, Mrs. Doe, your balance, which has been past due for over three months now.

Voice: Oh, you must be calling my daughter-in-law. I am just visiting here.

At this point the collector can only hope that the situation is not completely out of hand. One does not know the relationship between Mrs. Doe, Senior, and her daughter-in-law, but there is certainly a possibility that the collector has created a situation which could very well have been avoided had he been more careful to learn the exact identity of the person on the other end of the line. Conceivably the situation created in this example might be favorable for collection, but it should not have been precipitated accidentally.

Another excerpt from a collection call may illustrate the point further.

Collector: Could I speak with John Jones, please?

Voice: No John Jones lives here.

Collector: Is this Whitehall 0–0000?

Voice: Yes, this is Whitehall 0-0000.

Collector: Is your address 1111 Nowhere Drive?

Voice: Yes, that's right.

Collector: Do you know Mr. John Jones? It is very important that I reach him. I'm calling on a medical matter.

Voice: What kind of a medical matter?

Collector: Why, a bill he owes to Dr. Smith.

Voice: Well, that bill's been paid.

Collector: Then you do know Mr. John Jones?

Voice: Yes, I'm his wife, but he doesn't live here any more.

Although this call was obviously made by an agency collector, it illustrates the time that can be wasted and the lack of communication which can occur if the parties to the conversation do not know each other. It would have been much simpler if the conversation had gone something like this:

Collector: May I speak with Mr. John Jones, please?

Voice: No John Jones lives here.

Collector: To whom am I speaking, please?

Voice: This is Mrs. John Jones.

The practice of identifying the person at the other end of the line not only avoids unnecessary conversation, waste of time, and embarrassing situations, but it also enables you to call the other party by name. Being able to call the other party by his name gives you a definite psychological advantage in obtaining cooperation and information. It is much easier to be rude or uncooperative if one is anonymous. When our identity is unknown, we can indulge in behavior of which we would be ashamed if it were known to others. Thus knowledge of the other person's identity limits his freedom of action and gives you a degree of control over his behavior. If you know your respondent's name, he is much more likely to answer in a polite and conventional manner.

Also, use of the other person's name is an implied compliment. It tells him that he was important enough for you to make the effort to learn and to remember who he is. People like to have you catch their names and they like to be addressed by them. You should not only make it a practice to identify everyone with whom you speak, but you should also find occasions to use the name. It creates a warmer relationship.

2. *Use titles*

When talking with other individuals, customers or not, you should use titles. Address all persons as Mr., Mrs., or Miss. If some other title, such as Dr., or Judge, is appropriate, use it. Be liberal with the respectful "Sir." This not only underlines the formality and seriousness of the matter; it discourages the other person from assuming an intimacy toward you and, in addition, subtly flatters him. If you are talking to a customer, it emphasizes the fact that you are treating him like a responsible adult. You can, therefore, legitimately expect him to behave like one. If you take a condescending or patronizing tone, on the other hand, you invite immature and irresponsible behavior, which is precisely what you do not want.

3. *Assume the response you want*

In your conversations, both with the customer and with other persons you should phrase questions and comments in a form which invites the response you want. To a very large extent people act as others expect them to act. The minister gives up the argyle socks and plaid sports jackets after college graduation not so much because his tastes have changed as because people expect him to dress more soberly in his new role. We reply to the question, "How are you?" with, "Fine, thanks, and you?" neither because we are feeling well nor because we have a vital interest in the well-being of the interrogator. We do it because it is the reply expected and because it requires less effort than any other. It is easier to agree with others and to go along than it is to disagree and go against the current. Resistance requires effort. You should take a positive attitude which assumes that the other person will act as you want him to act.

For example, the question, "You don't happen to know his address, do you?" invites a negative reply, which you do *not* want. The simple demand, "Give me his address, please?" is just as courteous and assumes both cooperation and the answer you want. When put in this form, it is slightly more difficult for the individual to refuse the information and the burden is on the respondent. He has to make an effort in order to act contrary to your implied expectation. The response, "Then I will expect your check for the full amount by Friday," is a positive statement. The response, "And how much will that payment be for, sir?" fails to assume what you want. Both remarks tell the other person what you expect him to do. The first form clearly indicates that he should send his remittance for the full amount. If he is not going to do so, he will feel under some pressure to explain himself, and he will anticipate opposition. It is much easier just to assent. The second form just as clearly tells him that you do not expect the full amount. If you expect no more than a partial payment, why should he pay more?

When dealing with a prospective employer in trying to arrange an appointment, it may be all right to say, "What time would be convenient for you?" When dealing with a delinquent customer this is not all right. You should specify a time for the appointment and, if the time is not satisfactory, make adjustments. Do not ask the customer, "Would you give me your employer's name, please?" This anticipates the possibility of a refusal. Either the simple demand, "Tell me where you work," or "Who is your employer?" produces better results. "Will you put a check in the mail on Friday?" is not as positive as, "I will mark my records and expect your check on Monday." Whatever action you are trying to get out of the person on the other end of the line, you will do best if you phrase your remarks as if you expected no opposition or refusal, but rather expected cooperation and assent.

The principle is so important that it has been expanded by the famous Elmer Wheeler into what is virtually a whole new school of salesmanship. Some of us can remember when the gasoline attendant said, "How many gallons?" instead of "Fill 'er up, sir?" The day will come, I trust, when the question, "How much will that payment be?" will seem just as old-fashioned as. "How many gallons?"

4. *Do not give the customer excuses*

There is a corollary to this principle of making your requests and statements in a positive form. The corollary is to avoid suggesting answers you do not want. Do not put words in the other person's mouth or give him excuses he had not yet thought of. Remember, as a collector, you probably have a far better repertoire of excuses than any single customer has accumulated. Unfortunately, some of these illustrations are examples of actual blunders: "And you have no other source of income, Mr. Doe?" "You don't know where he moved to, sir?" "You can't possibly come in this week?" "These charges weren't incurred by you?" "Do you need more time?" "Would it be better if I called you next week?"

Each one of these might be rephrased. "What other income do you have, Mr. Doe?" "What is his new address, sir?" "When can you come in?" "The account is in your name." "The account is payable now." "I will call you on Monday."

It is impossible to anticipate all the ways in which a collector can cue others into responses which actually impede his efforts. The examples given are not far-fetched. They have been observed in the collection calls of highly trained and experienced collection men. They slip in insidiously. If there is any one fault which can be discovered in almost every collection conversation, it is either the failure to invite the response desired, or worse, the suggestion of an undesired response.

5. *Be sure he is listening*

Remember, in talking on the telephone, that someone must be listening before you can be heard. You must have the other person's attention. There is a common mistake which is made in this connection. Often people seem to be listening when they are really only awaiting their chance to speak. Give the customer his chance to talk, if only to be sure the channel is clear when you try to get your message across. If you do suspect that the other person is not listening to you, there is a way to check. You can simply mumble something incomprehensible and say, "That's right, isn't it?" If you get a "Yeah" or "Uh-huh," he was not listening. The person who is listening will ask what you said.

6. *Change to get attention*

Many people think that the only way to get attention is to raise one's voice or to speak more rapidly. As public speakers know, a more dramatic effect can sometimes be produced by a sudden drop in volume or a change to a slow and deliberate tempo. Any change in a situation demands attention. Those who live near elevated or subway lines soon become accustomed to the roar of the trains. A sudden silence can draw more attention than an increase in noise level. You can use the principle of change to call the attention of a customer to the things you have to say.

7. *Be brief*

Make your calls brief. Brevity in your phone calls permits you to make more of them. This has an advantage in itself. The more calls you make, the more you will collect. The basic message which you want to convey to the customer is a simple one. It is, simply, that you want payment and are concerned about the matter. This message does not require elaborate explanation. By the time you have identified yourself and stated your purpose in making the call, the customer has your message. Of course, you may add reasons for payment and other forms of persuasion to the basic message, but as you continue, you quickly run into a situation of diminishing returns.

Most of the arguments for immediate payment are already well-known to the credit customer. There really isn't too much you can say to make him feel guilty if he does not already feel slightly guilty. You cannot add appreciably to his anxiety about the matter if he is not already slightly apprehensive.

You achieve your maximum effect during the first few seconds on the telephone. The more the call is prolonged the less you achieve with additional time. Ten minutes is much better spent if it is divided into five separate conversations of two minutes each than if it is used in one extended period.

8. *Avoid argument*

Do not be led astray by the delusion that you are getting somewhere in an argument. Most people emerge from an argument remembering only those portions of the discussion which supported the beliefs they held before they went into it. Arguments are more likely to congeal and to fix previously held positions than they are to change them.

Not only do arguments accomplish little, but they use valuable time. They are frequently used by shrewd individuals to get you off the track. Unless you are careful, you can find yourself drawn into discussions about totally irrelevant matters. Keep your purpose firmly in mind. Remind yourself frequently that you want payment and that all else is beside the point.

9. *Get specific promises*

When you obtain a commitment from a customer, be sure you get him to make it specific. Force him to commit himself both as to the amount he will send and to the time it will be sent. You already have evidence that he is, to say the least, somewhat unreliable in the way he handles his obligations. If he were prompt, you would not be calling him. Pin the matter down and lock him into a specific promise. "O.K., I'll get it to you in a few days," does not mean any more than, "You must come over to my place for dinner sometime." You cannot get money over the telephone, so you must get the most definite and positive arrangements possible. Indicate to the customer that you are making a note of his commitment so that any delay or failure on his part will come to your attention.

10. *Follow up promises*

Be sure that you maintain an up-to-date tickler file on all collection activities. Prompt follow-up of all commitments is an absolute necessity. Failure to remind customers of their promises when they renege defeats your whole campaign of developing an atmosphere of urgency about the matter. Unless you treat the matter seriously, it is unlikely that the customer will consider it serious.

When you talked to the customer and obtained his promise to pay, he probably experienced certain feelings in a fairly well-defined sequence. Your call must have aroused some degree of concern. He at least cared enough about the matter to make you a promise. Making this promise got rid of you and brought him a feeling of relief. The behavior of making a promise was rewarded by this feeling of relief and will tend to be repeated in similar situations in the future. As time passes and the date for action on his promise draws near, the sight of a calendar, or the date on a newspaper, arouses feelings of concern again. He probably feels somewhat uncomfortable. If he obtains a money order or sends a check, he is again relieved. If he does not, some slight feelings of tension may remain as he worries about what you will do. If nothing happens, he experiences a feeling of relief without paying. The behavior of failing to keep a promise, then, is rewarded. This behavior gains an additional tendency to occur again in similar circumstances.

Failure to follow up is an excellent means of teaching already unreliable people to be more unreliable.

In almost all collection calls the customer can be expected to have some unpleasant feelings. If he has learned even a few of the basic lessons of socialization, your call stimulates some feelings of worry and concern. Whatever happens during that call at least removes one source of worry from the customer's scene. Getting rid of you is, to some extent, getting away from the debt. The minute the connection is broken, the immediate stimulus for keeping the matter in mind is gone. Whatever your effect may have been, it does not last long. People find ways to defend themselves from unpleasant feelings. They cannot long tolerate a mood of worry and concern. The customer may send you a check and thus get rid of these unpleasant feelings. He may engage in some other activity to take his mind off the subject. He is most unlikely to brood about it for a long time.

11. *Be persistent*

This leads to *the most important principle* of all collection effort—the need for persistence and repeated contacts.

Successive efforts have a cumulative effect. The debtor will forget his obligation if you permit it. This cumulative effect is more pronounced if repeated contacts are fairly close to one another in time. Allowing the matter to ride for several weeks or a month permits the effect of each contact to drop to zero, leaving nothing to build upon in your subsequent appeals. Not only does the effect drop to zero; it may go even beyond and build a negative force, a resistance to payment. The customer is allowed to experience a nice, long period of freedom from care as a result of ignoring your demands. This is definitely a rewarding situation which can make further collection efforts difficult. Behavior which is rewarded tends to be repeated. This cannot be said too often. You must be careful to observe what kinds of behavior you are rewarding for your credit customers.

12. *Keep control of the situation*

It is important that the collector keep control of the conversation. He has the initiative at the beginning because he establishes the purpose and sets the tone. He knows more about what is going to happen than does the customer. If the collector allows this control to slip from his hands, the customer may seize it and put the collector on the defensive. Such remarks as, "You must be new there," or "How old are you, young man?" are gambits used by some persons in an attempt to seize the offensive. Your newness, age, or experience are irrelevant issues. If you keep your purpose in mind, and treat such personal thrusts as beside the point, you will fare better than if you react to them. To the first remark one can answer simply, "The policy of our company has not changed." You would follow this up with a restatement of the terms of the account and return to the central issue by again asking for payment. To the second remark, it is merely necessary to state that your age is not the subject of the conversation. "We are discussing your past due account." You must not allow these personal challenges to succeed in their purpose. That purpose, of course, is to remove the topic into an arena where the customer has a better chance of success.

13. *Use motivating appeals*

The purposes of your call and the psychological effects of the call are very important, but there must be some content in what you say to the customer. In other words, you must give him some reason for paying, other than the fact that you want your money.

The same two groups of appeals that are used in collection by mail are also used in telephone collection, those based on the sense of "ought" and those based on avoidance. You have a somewhat wider choice in the range of themes you may draw from, but the motivations are the same. When you are appealing to the sense of "ought" you are attempting to arouse either a sense of guilt or a feeling of shame. The former is because the customer knows he is doing wrong, and the latter because others know or may know of his transgression.

When appealing to the sense of "ought," your suggestions may usually be a little balder and direct on the telephone than on paper. It would be difficult, for example, to design a notice which would shame a customer into paying by suggesting that his children might consider him a poor example. This can be implied, on occasion, in a telephone conversation. If you are trying to arouse his feelings of guilt, you can indulge in a little flattery by which you build up the image of his self-respect, his high standards, and his integrity. Then you can point out that the idea of evading debt is so contrary to this image that the contrast is painfully evident. You can, perhaps, assume that he is worried about the debt and talk about the relief he will feel when it is taken care of. You have a much wider latitude on the telephone than in a letter.

Even on the telephone, though, it is best to make your appeals to avoidance rather guarded. A threat, if it is made, must be followed up. As in poker, if you are caught in a bluff, you lose. Further, you run the risk of arousing stubborn pride. If your appeal is going to make reference to loss of credit standing, the possibility of contacting the debtor's employer, or legal action, these actions should either be only vaguely implied or you should make your meaning very clear and follow it up with action. The latter procedure, the direct threat to institute legal action, refer to an agency, get in touch with his employer, or take other steps, should be a last-ditch measure to be used only after all else has failed.

It is felt that the rules and principles of telephone collection which have been discussed have a general application to a diversity of collection problems. They will not, however, apply themselves. Collecting and reading about collecting are drastically different activities. In the final analysis, collecting skills are learned by collecting. Translating knowledge into skill requires the building of habits. Habits are formed by a diligent and conscious process of self-correction and practice. In brief, it is not enough to know how it ought to be done; you have to practice doing it.

COLLECTION BY A THIRD PARTY

XII

COLLECTION BY A THIRD PARTY

There comes a time when the credit granter should abandon his efforts to collect an account. In practice, the time when pursuit is abandoned is usually determined for each account either by the judgment of some person who is assigned that responsibility, or set for all delinquent accounts according to certain rules which are incorporated in the credit policy. Both in the use of judgment and in the application of rules, the credit granter takes into consideration such factors as the age of the account and its size. When abandonment of pursuit is the result of individual decisions, other items may affect the disposition of accounts. The past paying performance of the debtor, his occupation, nature of the merchandise sold, etc., may all affect these decisions.

Both use of judgment and application of rules, and all the variations and combinations of the two, are attempts to reach an economic decision. The credit granter does not want to continue to spend money in fruitless effort nor does he want to forfeit an opportunity to salvage the account for want of a little extra effort. He aims to cease his efforts when pursuit is no longer profitable.

Although the future of any individual delinquent account cannot be predicted with certainty, the outcomes of large numbers may be determined with something resembling mathematical precision. Although life insurance companies do not know which ones of their policyholders will die in any given year, they can predict how many will do so with extreme accuracy. Likewise, it is possible to forecast the behavior of delinquent accounts so that you can determine when the unprofitable point has been reached.

Basic Elements of Profitable Collection

Two basic elements enter into this computation: the costs of collection and the probability of collecting. The more accurately you know your collection costs and the more accurately you can estimate the probability of collecting, the more precise will be your determinations. Although your collection costs can be known, depending on the refinement and accuracy of your accounting procedures, the probability of collection will always be an estimate.

Probability always refers to events in the future, but it can be inferred only from the events of the past. You can estimate the probability of future collections from your past experience with comparable accounts. The proportion of similar accounts which you have collected in the past, expressed as a decimal fraction, can be taken as an estimate of the probability of collecting in the future. This is true only if you do not change your procedures and if other relevant factors remain constant.

The ways in which the past accounts are similar to those whose future you want to predict is important. They should be similar in ways which are relevant to their chances of being collected. It would not make much sense, for example, to estimate the probability of collecting the accounts of all persons whose last name begins with the letter "C" from your experience with such persons in the past. Initial letter of the name has little bearing on collectibility of accounts. It would be better to estimate the probability of collecting accounts over six months of age from your experience with accounts of that age in the past. The age of the account is related to its collectibility.

In general, the larger the group of past accounts on which you can base your estimates of probability, the more reliable will be those estimates. For the usual credit granter this fact poses limitations. If he wants to know, for example, the probability that he will collect an account which is exactly four months delinquent, is exactly $37.50 in amount, and is owed by someone living in an apartment, he is unlikely to have enough similar accounts to give him any reliable estimates. He can, however, usually find enough data to give him a reasonable estimate of the probability of collecting accounts which are over four months delinquent.

Determining How Much Your Accounts Are Worth

The next step, after an estimate of probability is obtained, is to compute your mathematical expectancy of gain. The mathematical expectancy of gain is very simply the probability of collecting, multiplied by the amount of the account. For example, if you estimate the probability of collecting an account at 0.1, because you have collected 10 per cent of similar accounts in the past, and the amount of the account is $10, your mathematical expectancy is $1. Or, if you have collected half of comparable accounts in the past, you would estimate your probability of collection at 0.5. Your mathematical expectancy would be $5 for an account of $10.

Your mathematical expectancy does not, of course, tell you how much you should expect to get out of any one particular account. The future of an individual account is not predictable. With respect to any one given account you are most likely to collect the whole amount or nothing at all. Your mathematical expectancy tells you that, if you had large groups of similar accounts, your best guess about the *average* expected gain would be the amount computed by multiplying the amount of the account by its probability of collection. It gives you an estimate of your recovery over the long run.

Let us apply these ideas to a simplified but specific situation.

Suppose that the accounts on which you must reach a decision are all of $25 balances and that your mark-up was $5 on each. In this case, your actual loss would be $20 on each account if you failed to collect anything. We will further assume that, because of your experience with similar accounts, you have estimated the probability of collection to be 0.25; that is, you prophesy that you will collect one-fourth of the accounts.

If you write off the accounts without further collection effort, your average loss will be $20 per account plus any collection expense already incurred. Since the collection expense already incurred is a constant factor throughout all your possible alternatives, it will be neglected. It is an additional loss no matter what you decide to do.

Since you have estimated the probability of collection as 0.25, you will expect to recover 0.25 times $25, or $6.25, per account. This recovery would reduce your average loss to $13.75 ($20 minus $6.25) to which loss must be added the costs of the further collection effort. If that effort should cost you only $6.25 per account, your loss is right back up to $20 per account, and you have done a lot of work with no result other than, perhaps, to educate your customers. If the costs of additional collection effort exceed your mathematical expectancy of gain, you will lose money by continuing to try to collect.

Let us assume that you are considering referring your accounts to a third party for collection. You will want to know what per cent you can expect the third party to recover. Recovery rates vary widely as a function of the type of account, age of the account at placement, amount of previous collection effort expended, and a number of other factors. Actually, there is no recovery rate which can be considered typical. You will have to find out the probability of agency collection in the same way that you made your predictions about your own probability of collection; that is, by past experience.

We will assume, however, that you know of an agency which collects 40 per cent of the same kind of accounts of which you expect only to collect 25 per cent. Although 40 per cent is not an unusual recovery rate, it is selected arbitrarily merely because it is above the 25 per cent we have assumed for the probability of internal collection.

Let us further assume that this agency also charges 40 per cent of whatever it collects for such accounts. This is not an unusual rate. Under these two assumptions, you would expect the agency to recover an average of $10 for each $25 account. This is its mathematical expectancy—0.4 times $25. Since it keeps 40 per cent of what it collects and returns 60 per cent to you, you would receive an average of $6 per account after the commission had been deducted. Your loss is reduced to $14 flat ($20 minus the recovered $6). All the costs of collection have been included in the commision. If you know your collection costs, you can make a fairly good estimate of when you should refer your accounts to a third party for collection. The agency's recovery rate multiplied by the percentage of collections, which are returned to you after the commission has been deducted, yields your net expectancy from referral. If, for example, the agency can produce a 40 per cent recovery rate and charges you a commission of 40 per cent, you will expect a net recovery of 60 per cent of the 40 per cent (0.6 x 0.4) or about 24 per cent. In this example, the agency could be expected to produce a *net* recovery of 24 per cent while continued effort without referral would be expected to produce a *gross* recovery of 25 per cent. From this gross recovery you would have to deduct the costs of further collection effort to find the net recovery.

When to Abandon Your Collection Effort

It is when the mathematical expectancy from internal efforts is slightly higher than that from referral that the costs of collection effort become crucial. There is some point at which your *gross* recovery would be greater than the *net* recovery from an agency but your *net* recovery would be less than that of the agency. Your collection costs make the difference in the net recovery rates.

This is the most profitable time for referral, i.e., when your collection costs make your net expected recovery less than that to be expected from an agency.

Public Relations and the Third Party

Economic considerations are not the only ones which should influence decisions on referral of accounts to a third party. You have the matter of public relations to consider. This is an important consideration for any businessman, although perhaps more important to some than to others. If collection efforts on difficult accounts are ever to be successful, it is quite possible that some plain talk to the credit customer may be required. Plain talk, however courteously phrased, runs the risk of arousing the customer's hostility. The anger will most likely be directed toward the one who did the talking. If you did the talking, you will bear the brunt. If a collection agency did it, then the collection agency takes the blame. If some of the hostility does spill over to your company, you can always blame the agency. This tactic is known widely as "passing the buck" and agencies are accustomed to taking the blame.

If matters go to the point where the only thing that will move the customer is a talk with his employer, it may often be better from a public relations viewpoint to let an agency do the talking than to do it yourself. If a customer has broken promises to you, perhaps an agency can be firmer in its insistence on performance than you would care to be. This does not mean that you should look for an agency to do your dirty work; it does mean that you might wish to employ an agency to handle your delicate work. A good agency can help rather than hurt your public relations.

Disadvantages of Write-off

You may be tempted to think that you would do best just to write off your accounts and not to refer them to a third party for collection. There are disadvantages to this procedure beyond the loss of money to the owners of your business.

1. A customer who is delinquent in his obligations to you is often too embarrassed to continue doing business with you. This does not mean, however, that he does not continue to have needs for the services or goods you supply. It

does mean that he will be more likely to satisfy his needs with your competitors simply because he dreads facing his problem. If he can get out of his predicament, you have a chance to return him to your roster of active customers even if only on a cash basis.

2. Further, unwillingness to take all possible steps to effect collection is a policy which eventually becomes known to chronic debtors who begin to favor you with their patronage. This kind of reputation can increase collection costs and loss from bad debt. You can do very well without this kind of credit customer.

3. Last, you are not being fair to your responsible customers. Why should they pay when you do not make every effort to collect from others? Such a policy, if it becomes known, can cause your good customers to become resentful and to wonder to what extent *their* prices include *your* credit losses. Many people of sound financial status conscientiously avoid doing business with companies with liberal credit policies because they expect high credit losses to result and to be passed on to them. Responsible people who regard their credit as "good as cash" do not expect to pay a premium for credit privileges.

When to Place With a Collection Agency

It has probably become clear that placement with an agency is advocated. My preference for this action rather than direct referral to an attorney may be the result of prejudice. Nevertheless, I believe I have reasons for this position. The collection of most delinquent accounts appears to be more of a psychological problem than a legal one. It is a matter of applying psychological pressures to induce the customer to pay his obligations without recourse to legal action. Collection through legal processes is expensive, time consuming, and eventually harmful to the customer. Collection without suit is far better for all concerned.

Relatively few delinquent accounts actually require suit. There are a great many steps between the point where it is expedient for the credit granter to quit and the point at which all alternatives except suit have been exhausted. Some of these steps are discussed in the following chapter. It is true that many accounts are settled because legal action is threatened, but an agency, too, can state that the credit granter will file suit.

It is always possible to file suit through an attorney after the agency has exhausted all other forms of persuasion. Referral to an attorney for suit short-circuits these intermediate appeals. It is much as if, in the earlier stages of your collection procedure, you went directly from a first to a final notice.

Of course, there are attorneys who are expert collectors, and this discussion does not refer to them. It is contended that referring accounts for suit as soon as you have exhausted your appeals is not the best collection policy. For this reason all subsequent discussion of third parties will refer to agencies although it will include those attorneys who specialize in collection by persuasion as well as suit.

How to Select an Agency

Whatever third party you decide to use for the collection of your delinquent accounts, you should remember that this person or company will be handling your money. Further, the collection agency may be held to be acting as your agent, in which case you are responsible for its actions. Your choice of agency will make a considerable difference in the results you obtain.

As you examine collection agencies, you will find that some have advantages over others. Of course, you want accurate accounting of funds collected for you. You want prompt remittance of the portion of those collections due you. You want your customers handled humanely. You want service for any special requests you may make. And you want a satisfactory recovery rate. Perhaps you will be able to find all of these things in one agency. The chances are that there will be some aspect of the service of any agency which will be inferior to that of another agency. One agency may be inclined to be a little bit delayed in making its remittances, but when remittances are received you find them absolutely accurate. Another agency may make occasional errors in its reports, but you find it absolutely prompt with remittances. This is nothing unusual. You find such differences in all the companies with whom you do business. You will, of course, choose the agency with better service in the areas which are most important to you.

Check financial statements

As you evaluate services, however, you must not lose sight of the fact that your agency is acting in a fiduciary capacity to you. The most important element for you to consider is the financial integrity of the company you select. It does not matter how much an agency collects if you cannot get remittances from them. Financial integrity can be inferred to some extent from financial statements. But, probably the best indicator of integrity will be found in a long record of ethical dealings with other credit granters.

Obtain references

You should ask for references from any agency you are considering. Obtain the names of other companies and professional people for whom they are collecting, and check with these credit granters for references. Ask if the agency is prompt with remittances, if discrepancies have been discovered in reports, whether they have had complaints from customers, and if the recovery rate is satisfactory.

Visit offices

If possible, you should visit the offices of any collection agency being considered. By such a visit you get an idea of the type of operation it conducts and the caliber of the people it employs. Such personal impressions can be invaluable both in helping you to make your decision and in your later relations with the agency.

Check for memberships

Membership in such trade associations as the Associated Credit Bureaus of America, the American Collectors Association, Chambers of Commerce, and Better Business Bureaus, are favorable indicators. However, trade associations, depending as they do upon the cooperation and good will of their members, are limited in the pressures they can exert on individuals in their organizations. Such memberships usually indicate only that the member has met certain minimum requirements. Membership does not guarantee superior qualifications.

Inquire about bonding

Since the employees of your collection agency will be handling funds belonging to you, they should be bonded, and you should inquire about this point. If some of your accounts are to be forwarded to agencies in other parts of the country, you will want to know if any losses sustained as a result of the actions of these other agencies are also covered. Such losses are covered for all members of the American Collectors Association through a bond provided by that organization.

John W. Johnson, Executive Secretary of the American Collectors Association, makes the following observations on the selection of a collection agency:

1. We usually recommend that businessmen deal with a local, well established collector . . . and not one who operates out of a distant city. The reasons are that the creditor is able to establish a close working relationship with his collector and is able to be familiar with the collector's procedures, should he want this information.

The collector is also much more familiar with local conditions, such as unemployment, strikes, plant layoffs, rehirings, physical employment pickup, etc., which allow him to work the accounts more intelligently and know when they are likely to be collectible.

The local collector also is likely to become more acquainted with many of the habitual local debtors and is more likely to know what is necessary to make collection.

There are other reasons plus these which can be elaborated upon.

2. He should show evidence of having complied with any state or local bonding or licensing provisions. This is merely to show that the collector is permanent and serious about being in the business.

In several states, such as Minnesota, for example, the law requires agencies to carry a bond but it has no enforcement provisions; consequently, collectors can operate without complying with state law unless someone gets the local county attorney to take action on his complaint to enforce compliance.

These laws also are set up to protect the creditors in most cases, and the creditor should know what avenues of protection accorded him by law have met compliance.

3. He should be a member of an international trade association, such as the American Collectors Association. This allows him to give the creditor personal collection coverage through affiliated members against debtors no matter where they may now be located.

It also assures the creditor he has met a certain basic set of requirements and that he maintains a basic minimum level of operation to retain his membership.

It also assures the creditor that his collector has available to him up-to-date programs of collection techniques, procedures, etc., so that 'modern service' can be provided.

4. Reputation. One of the most important ways to select a collector is by checking those for whom he personally does collection work. If his business references are good, the creditor has pretty good assurance that he will be satisfied.

5. Finally, we recommend that creditors make a personal visit to the collector's office, just to see his business setup, look at some of his form letters, etc., to satisfy himself that he is making a good choice and that he can put complete confidence in the collector thereafter.*

It is recommended that you deal with only one agency rather than with several. There are a number of reasons for this recommendation. In the first place, your accounting is simplified both with respect to the receipt of money and with respect to the referral of delinquent accounts. You always know who has any particular account and you always know who collected it. A more important reason is that your collection agency should become, in effect, an extension of your own credit department. This does not mean that you should exercise

* John W. Johnson, in a personal letter to the author, dated June 17, 1960.

close supervision over its efforts, but that you should work in close cooperation with it. Your agency needs from you every bit of information which comes in. If you get information about a change of address, relay it. If you happen across new employment information, give it to the agency. They want to collect for you. Help them to do so.

Do not burden your agency with requests for progress reports. It is geared to collection work, not reporting. If you have chosen a reputable agency, there is little need for close control. You should be able to trust it or you should not be using its services.

How Agencies Charge

Most agencies accept accounts for collection on a contingent fee basis, that is to say, "no collection, no charge." They charge a commission only on funds actually collected. There is no charge on accounts which you list and on which the agency does not obtain results. When you consider the commission charged on the accounts collected, you should bear in mind the others on which the agency has worked but which are "for free" to you. Whether the accounts are paid to you or paid to the agency, the agency expects its commission. You should, of course, be prompt to notify it of any payments received by you on accounts which have been placed with the agency. You will want it to discontinue efforts on these accounts both in fairness to the debtor and in fairness to the agency.

Contingent fee commissions charged by agencies range from about 25 per cent to about 50 per cent. Usually there is a differential provided in the rates calling for higher commissions in certain special cases. Older accounts, accounts previously handled by other agencies, accounts which require legal action, or those on which you cannot furnish a valid current address are among those on which your agency may ask a premium. Even with these exceptions, the fee will very seldom be in excess of 50 per cent.

On the financial side, you should not judge an agency from the size of its commission alone. If your agency charges, for example, 40 per cent of the money recovered and recovers 50 per cent of the accounts listed, you are getting 60 per cent of the 50 per cent or a net return of 30 per cent on your listed accounts. Another agency may charge only 25 per cent, but collect only 30 per cent. Your net yield in the latter case is 75 per cent of the 30 per cent or only 22½ per cent. Clearly the advantage in such a case is with the more "expensive" agency. With collection agencies as with other services, you often get just what you pay for. It is your net recovery, after commission, which is the important factor on the money side.

Perhaps, though, it is worthwhile to caution you that it is possible to produce a higher recovery rate at a cost you would not want to pay. It is possible to be brutal with debtors and thereby to increase a recovery rate by a few percentage points. It is doubtful if the few extra dollars gained by such a procedure is worth the damage either to your company's reputation or the damage to one's own self-respect. You should listen to and investigate complaints about agency tactics, remembering that most of the reports you receive are biased. Keep an open mind, but be sure that you are neither encouraging nor condoning irresponsible badgering of debtors, worthy or unworthy. The end does not justify the means either in collection or in police enforcement.

Some few agencies have departed from the usual contingent fee basis in their charges to some claimants. This is a relatively new trend and is being extended by only a few agencies to only a few claimants. It is quite possible that the trend will grow. These few agencies offer to handle all collections of, or over, a certain age for a flat monthly fee. Arrangements are made with individual claimants for the amount of this fee based on the volume and value of their credit business and prior collection experience. At the present time, this type of contractual arrangement does not appear to be generally available.

Both arrangements have their advantages. The contingent fee basis is an arms-length arrangement in which the credit granter pays only for known results. The contract arrangement is one in which the agency and the credit granter must have faith in one another. As agencies become better known and more highly respected, one would expect the latter arrangement to increase in popularity.

Services of Agencies

Some agencies offer a free dunning letter or notice to their claimants as a service. These free letters are sent to the debtor by you and usually inform him that the account will be placed with the agency if payment is not received in your office by a certain deadline. Of course, the agency expects you to follow through on your commitment and place the account for collection if the debt is not liquidated by the deadline specified.

Many agencies offer a service which passes by a variety of names, but which is, in essence, a letter service. The agency contracts to send some specified number of letters or notices to the debtor within a given period of time. These letters urge the debtor to pay you directly. This type of service is usually available at a much lower contingent fee than the regular collection service, because the agency expects you to place the accounts with it for regular collection service if the effort is not successful, and because an automatic series of letters with all remittances made to you is less expensive for the agency.

This service is an excellent one for the small credit granter who does not employ specialized collectors. It puts the same kind of mail pressures on the debtors which are employed by the larger credit granters. It is of dubious value to the larger credit granter whose accounts have already gone beyond the stage where impersonal efforts are likely to get results. If the accounts have already been thoroughly worked by collectors, they should probably receive individual attention from an agency at the earliest time possible.

Other Agency Practices

Cancellation

You, of course, have the right to cancel any account which has been placed with an agency. It is only fair to the agency, however, to keep cancellations to a minimum. Remember, the agency makes an investment in every account that it lists. It has incurred expenses in typing, filing, mailing, and telephoning. It charges you for only those accounts on which it collects. The ones which are not collected represent pure expense. Cancellations, therefore, cost the agency money. Certainly you should not cancel an account if the debtor pays you immediately after you receive an acknowledgment from the agency. Very probably the debtor recived a notice from the agency at the same time you got the acknowledgment. The debtor may very well have paid you as a result of that notice.

Who gets paid first?

The agency probably has other accounts listed against many of the individuals from whom you are asking it to collect. A large proportion of the names listed in the files of a collection agency are those of people who are delinquent in their accounts with a number of creditors. This is one of the advantages the agency has over the individual credit granter; it has more of the story.

Ordinarily, the agency will collect these accounts in the order in which they were listed. If you are the first to list an account against Richard Roe, for example, you will be the first creditor to be paid from the money it collects from him. It is clearly to your advantage to refer an account promptly when you have reason to believe that the debtor has gotten in too deeply with too many different creditors.

There is an exception to this policy which is followed by a number of agencies. If there is difficulty in locating a debtor and there are multiple claims against him, the order of payment may be altered to favor the creditor who gives a current address and makes it possible to obtain payment for all the others who also have claims.

Debt consolidation

The accumulation of debts for the same individual can enable the agency collector, who knows more about the debtor's position, to talk with him in terms of consolidation of his obligations. Perhaps he can arrange for the debtor to get a loan so that all his creditors may be paid at the same time. This, of course, takes each creditor out of the finance business into which such debtors have put him.

If you conduct a credit operation, you will inevitably meet with accounts which resist your best efforts to collect. In fairness to your other customers and the owners of the business, every step which is economically possible should be taken to enforce collection. These steps are not complete until the account has been referred to a third party. It is possible to make the referral at a time which will produce the best net recovery. Third party collection can actually improve rather than injure your public relations if care is exercised in the selection of an agency. Although a number of factors should be considered in making your selection, chief among them are integrity and net recovery. Third party collection is an important last step in the collection campaign.

COLLECTION BY AGENCY

XIII

COLLECTION BY AGENCY

The collection agency uses essentially the same techniques as those used by the credit granter. The difference between the two is not so much a difference in methods as it is a difference in the roles and attitudes of the agency collector as contrasted with the company collector. The appeals are similar, but the urgency is increased. The persistence is more apparent. The tone is more demanding.

Appeals and Techniques of Agencies

Like the creditor, the agency tries to stimulate the debtor by appealing to his sense of "ought" and to his desire to avoid unpleasant consequences. The agency is more inclined to emphasize appeals based on avoidance. It assumes that the credit granter has already made a number of appeals to the debtor's feeling of obligation and duty and has found them fruitless.

The agency also uses the same means to reach the debtor with its appeals. Notices and letters are sent through the mail and telephone calls are made. The agency, however, makes its chief effort by means of telephone in order to step up the atmosphere of urgency.

The Outside Collector

The outside collector—who is the typical bill collector in the popular mind—is virtually extinct. Outside collectors are seldom used either by credit granters or by collection agencies. This is partly because of economic developments which make the personal call on the debtor too expensive for wide use. The rising level of wage rates applies to the bill collector as well as to other occupations. The number of personal calls an individual collector can make in the course of a day's work, even in areas of heavy debtor concentration, is severely limited. When the daily wage is divided by the number of calls, each call can be seen to represent a considerable investment. Since only a fraction of these investments yields returns, the personal collection call becomes an extremely expensive procedure.

It has also been found that, in the large majority of cases, a telephone approach to the debtor is as effective, and sometimes more effective, than is the personal call. If it is necessary to see the debtor in person, it is more to the collector's advantage to see him in his own office. When the interview takes place in the office of the collector, the collector is on his home ground, he feels more at ease, the situation is a familiar one to him, and he is in control. If the collector must talk with the debtor in the debtor's home, the debtor is in a better position to try to assume command. He not only feels more secure in his own home than in the agency, but he is also in a better position to direct the course of events. The debtor can terminate discussion, if that course appears desirable to him, or he can arrange matters so that they distract the collector, appeal to his sympathy, or merely annoy him. The collector can be at a definite disadvantage when he must talk with the debtor at the debtor's home while he has equally distinct advantages when the conversation can be held in his own office. If a chance for collection exists, there is seldom a case in which the proper approach cannot induce the debtor to come to the office of the agency. Outside collection efforts are seldom really necessary.

Advantages of the Agency

Although the methods of the agency and the creditor are similar, the agency has certain advantages. The agency collector is able to take a somewhat different attitude. In the first place, since the credit granter has given up, the collector is in a position to be more severe in his approach to the debtor. Like the school principal to whom the teacher has referred a disciplinary problem, he can begin his efforts with a presumption of guilt. The debtor is in the wrong or the account would not have been referred for collection. The debtor has had more than enough time to complain about the goods or services and to seek an adjustment. The account has been due long enough for the debtor to have accumulated the money to pay it if he had that intention. The agency collector does not need to ask, indeed he should not ask, for excuses. He can presume that the account would not be in his hands if there were valid excuses.

The agency collector is in a position to insist on immediate payment, payment today, not tomorrow or next payday, but before five o'clock this afternoon. The debtor will see nothing out of character in an agency collector who makes such demands. The business of an agency is collection, and it seems more appropriate for an agency collector to insist that the matter must be cleared up without delay than it does for the creditor to whom collection is a subsidiary activity. The agency makes its money by collecting, and it wants to get the business transacted. This difference in point of view is perceived by many debtors, and they react to it. Of course, the agency collector may not get his payment by five o'clock, but the fact that he is in a position to talk in such terms places an emphasis on time which it is difficult for the creditor to achieve. After such a firm insistence on the urgency of payment now, any extension of time granted by the agency collector is likely to be felt to be a major concession.

Again, because of the way the debtor sees the agency, the agency collector's demand for payment of the entire balance in full is more convincing than would be a similar demand by the creditor. The debtor usually believes, rightly or wrongly, that he can appease the creditor with a token payment of some amount less than the full balance. The belief that he has this option is comforting, because, if the pressure becomes too great, he feels he can buy more time with a relatively small part of what is owed. When the agency collector says, "We're not in the installment business. We want payment in full, today!" the matter has become more serious. The debtor is no longer so confident that he has the option of partial payment and, if he is able to gain a respite with less than the full amount, he is more eager to take the opportunity. Now, he may feel that it is a privilege to be able to reduce the pressure with a partial payment.

Because of its role, the collection agency can be less covert and less diplomatic in suggesting that further delay will bring unpleasant consequences. The agency collector can state quite openly and without either sugar coating or apology that he will get in touch with the debtor's employer or that the creditor will start suit.

The agency often has another advantage arising from the fact that a number of different claims against the same individual may be in its hands at the same time. The agency collector is then in a position to know more nearly the full range of the debtor's difficulties. Under these circumstances, since the worst is known, some debtors will confess their predicaments. The agency collector is in a position to help them work out some budget arrangement or a consolidation of debts through a loan. Sometimes the debtor is simply ashamed to talk with his creditor, but he may be induced to talk openly to a third party. As irrational as such an attitude may seem, it is not infrequently encountered.

Last, the collection agency is made up of collection specialists. Their interests are not spread over the areas of marketing and public relations. Each day they deal with people who are in debt to the point that it has become a problem to their creditors, if not to themselves. The agency collector develops a "feel" for these problems and a mental "set" to collect. He does not have to switch his role. He practices his skills in one area of credit, that of collection.

The agency collector exploits these advantages in a number of specific ways. You will remember that he is dealing with persons who have won all of their bouts in the preliminaries. He is more aggressive, more authoritative, and more skeptical.

The agency collector takes the position that you, the claimant, are right and the debtor is wrong. If the debtor does have a case, he has to sell it to the collector. For example, if the debtor claims to have paid the account, the agency collector demands specific proof such as check or money order number, on whom it was drawn, to whom payable, amount, date, and endorsement information. He is likely to demand that the debtor bring his receipt or cancelled check to the office so that its authenticity may be verified.

If the debtor complains about the service or the merchandise, the collector finds it difficult to believe that adjustment or satisfaction could not have been obtained before the account was placed. Again, he demands proof and specific details.

Perhaps the debtor claims to have no income. The agency collector immediately wants to know how he lives, where he gets money for his food, his rent, etc. He wants to know how long he has been out of work, when he expects to go back, what kind of work he does, etc. If the debtor balks at giving him all this information, the collector challenges his sincerity. He keeps such debtors on the defensive with his attitude that they are in the wrong.

The agency collector does not ask *why* a debt has not been paid. This is an invitation to the debtor to offer excuses and implies that the excuses might be accepted instead of money. Although the agency collector listens to excuses, he does not ask for them. It establishes the wrong relationship from his point of view.

The agency collector insists on immediate action. If the debtor claims he does not have the money to pay it all today, he is apt to meet the blunt question, "When will you have it?" If he cannot specify a time, the collector may ask where he can borrow it: "Come now, Mr. Debtor, don't you have any relatives or friends?"

He is very clear on the point that neither the agency nor the claimant is in the finance business. He may inquire whether the debtor has any personal loans outstanding and may even go so far as to help him obtain one.

When the collector is forced to give an extension of time, he may do a little acting in which he pleads the debtor's case to an imaginary supervisor. After he has, with obvious difficulty, obtained this special concession for the debtor, he asks, "With whom are you employed?" or "What kind of work do you do?" The collector is always aware that he may need employment information for leverage, and, if the debtor resists giving him such information, he might say, "If your promise is sincere, you can't possibly be afraid I would call there or cause trouble. Honest people don't refuse to give this type of information."

Sometimes it is necessary to arrange terms. Here, too, the agency collector does the dictating. He will usually refuse to discuss terms on the telephone, but will insist that the debtor come to the office. When the debtor comes in, the collector learns as much about the debtor's financial situation as possible and discusses payment terms. Acting on the theory that most debtors offer less than they can afford to pay, the collector typically expresses dissatisfaction with the size of the first offer and asks for a larger one. He usually gets it. He next arranges the rest of the terms, makes out a note, passes it to the debtor and indicates where the debtor is to sign. He then puts the pen *into the debtor's hand*—not just in front of him. If he meets resistance, he backs up and starts again insisting on immediate payment in full.

The agency collector may not only state the consequences which the debtor will encounter if he does not pay but may also suggest such consequences indirectly. He may deliberately allow the debtor to hear side comments about garnishments, suits, or employers which he makes to a fictitious colleague, e.g., "Excuse me a moment, Mr. Debtor. Yeah, Joe. (pause) Oh, that one's all right. His boss said he'd either pay it today or he would let him go."

After a "staller" has completed his routine of complaints and excuses, the agency collector may get in touch with him a short while later about a claim from another credit granter. This makes it very difficult for the debtor to maintain the pose of an injured customer, a forgetful person, or a well-intentioned character in temporary difficulties. As the evidence of poor money management accumulates, there is increasing pressure on the debtor to make a clean breast of the full extent of his difficulties. As in other areas, admission and definition of the problem is necessary to solution. The naivete with respect to money matters which one encounters among otherwise knowledgeable and shrewd persons is nothing short of shocking. Once such persons drop their pretenses, it is not difficult to guide them.

The agency collector moves from collection problem to collection problem with a minimum of waste motion. His success depends on the number of debtors from whom he can collect, and he is well aware that number of collections depends on number of contacts. Since he deals only with problem cases, he becomes familiar with "dodges" and develops standard answers to them.

The debtor who is a "con artist" meets a skeptical adversary when he comes up against the agency collector, who has had people try the same line before and, probably, not more than a few hours *before*. Just as the company collector is "set" to expect honesty, so the agency collector is "set" to expect deceit.

Although the agency collector has no special magic to help him collect money, he has some definite advantages over the company collector. Chief among these advantages is his ability to adopt the attitude that the debtor is in the wrong. Because of the way the debtor perceives the agency's role, the collector can be more insistent on immediate payment and payment in full. Also because of the way the debtor perceives the agency, the collector can be balder in his use of appeals to avoidance. He has heard all of the subterfuges and has learned how to counter them. He exploits these advantages to bring stronger pressure on the debtor to pay.

SKIP TRACING

XIV

SKIP TRACING

Skip tracing is a fascinating and challenging activity. Locating an individual whose whereabouts is unknown requires ingenuity, imagination and persistence. It is a kind of detective work which, at its best, combines both thoroughness and inspiration. Although the cases in which a skip has been located through a single brilliant maneuver make the best anecdotes, no amount of cleverness can compensate for a lack of thoroughness. The patient and painstaking pursuit of all leads is the foundation on which most successful skip tracing is based.

General Sequence for Tracing

While a thoughtless plodding through a routine series of steps may appear to be thoroughness of a sort, it is not the kind of discriminating care which locates the maximum number of skips with the minimum amount of effort. The skip tracer should exercise judgment in selecting the more promising leads for earlier investigation. It is not necessary to follow any rigid pattern or sequence of steps. The investigation should proceed from those inquiries which are most likely to bear fruit to those which are less likely to do so.

There is a general order in the usual attempts to locate skips. Some leads are ordinarily more apt to yield information than are others, but they are not invariably more profitable. This general pattern of inquiry should be followed when none of the information available suggests a better approach. One should depart from it, too, when new information suggests a better line of inquiry. The goal of skip tracing is to locate and collect profitably. This goal should be attained by the fastest and least expensive route possible.

The factor of economy is an important one in skip tracing. At its cheapest, skip tracing is usually quite expensive. For smaller accounts it is often too expensive. Nevertheless, there is potential revenue in every account, and, if a little extra effort will salvage that revenue, the extra effort should be made.

Be objective

The decision as to whether to trace or not to trace an account is influenced by several factors. You should take into account the total profitability which could result from tracing. Profitability involves the potential revenue which could be gained, the probability of collecting after the debtor is located, the investment which has already been made in collection, and the costs of the tracing effort. Your decisions should be dispassionate and logical. They should not be biased by emotional factors. Collectors have failed to trace accounts when they should trace because they had an ample supply of easier accounts on which they preferred to work. Others have spent an unjustifiable amount of time and money on an account because they have become angry with a debtor. They have been carried away by their desire to "show" him. Make your judgments on a careful analysis of all the facts.

Kinds of Skips

One of the matters you will want to consider is the kind of skip you are tracing. A debtor is classified as a skip when he cannot be found at the address you have been given. All the debtors so classified, however, are not *intentional* skips. Some, in the haste of moving, have merely forgotten to leave a forwarding address. Others may have relied on someone else to take care of the forwarding. Sometimes the skip begins in this innocent manner but, as time goes by and nothing happens, he becomes more and more forgetful. Since no one noticed his failure to pay and drew his attention to it, the debt becomes less obligatory. Of course, there are some skips who did not intend to pay if they could get away without doing so. These are the credit criminals. However, you would make a big mistake if you treated all skips as if they were intentionally evading payment.

Two Basic Approaches

The kind of skip you are tracing would also influence the methods you might employ. There are two basic approaches to skip tracing.

One approach relies on subterfuge and deceit while the other is candid and straightforward. There are, of course, blends of the two approaches because there are degrees of candor and deceit. The skip tracer might be open and frank in his relations with one informant but be quite deceitful in his conversation with another. The use of subterfuge is more likely to be employed in an effort to track down the intentional skip—the credit criminal.

These persons are deliberately trying to defraud those whom they have induced to trust them. They are consciously trying to cheat their creditors. In doing so, they do not hesitate to lie or to use trickery. They go to great pains to cover their tracks. An open inquiry concerning them or their affairs is met with guile and evasion. An undisguised attempt to locate such persons stands no more chance of success than does an attempt to track and capture a fox without stealth.

In such circumstances the skip tracer resorts to subterfuge out of necessity. Otherwise his position would be much like that of a man who tries to observe the Marquis of Queensbury rules in a barroom brawl. The ethical problems concerning the use of subterfuge can be resolved by the same arguments which are used by police in undercover work or that nations advance to defend espionage. In such cases, it is felt, one must "fight fire with fire." The skip tracer who bays on the trail of a foxy credit criminal is simply foolish.

There are, however, borderline cases in which the intent of the skip is not so clearly fraudulent. Nevertheless uncamouflaged attempts to locate the skip are met with concealment and evasion. The solution to the ethical problem in such cases is not so apparent. If the purpose of tracing the skip is admitted to be a legitimate one, if the use of deceit will cause no harm or distress to others, and if it appears that the skip cannot be located otherwise—it would seem that subterfuge is justified.

Whenever ruses are used in the attempt to locate a skip, you should conscientiously consider the effect you may have on other persons. You should scrupulously avoid the use of any device or pretense which could conceivably harm any person or group. Do not descend to tactics which would cause emotional distress or shock to the person whom you are questioning. Further, of course, you should be careful not to violate the law. For example, you should never represent yourself as a government official of any kind.

Tracing With Subterfuge

Successful skip tracing through the use of subterfuge requires more than a knowledge of the "gags" and "gimmicks" by which one may obtain information. It requires skill in acting and impersonating. The most plausible ruse can be transparent if the skip tracer is not adept in creating the atmosphere and personality which make his story believable. Conversely, the adroit skip tracer can make highly improbable circumstances seem convincing. The roles the skip tracer adopts are not as important as is his art in playing the roles.

How to Use Gags and Gimmicks

There are numerous "gags" which have been adopted by professional skip tracers. Each has more or less favorite roles which he plays best. The skip tracer may become a truck driver who has just found a wallet belonging to the debtor. The wallet, of course, contains some money and the telephone number of the person the tracer is calling. Since the truck driver is only passing through town, it is important that he reach the debtor immediately. The skip tracer may be an insurance investigator checking on an application for group health insurance. He may be an insurance adjuster who wants to make payment on a claim. He might be in the personnel department of the skip's former employer. At income tax time he could be seeking the new address of the skip so he could mail his W-2 form to him. Naturally it was returned unclaimed from the former address. On another occasion the skip tracer might be a buddy from the debtor's days in the service. Perhaps he is just passing through town and wants to say hello for old time's sake. Maybe he wants to repay a loan, or strangely effective, he may be in desperate straits and want to make a "touch." He might still be in the service and be calling from a phone booth just before he is "shipped out." He might be anybody who could have a reasonable excuse for wanting to find the skip, but who needs to do it in a hurry.

It is the urgency of the need for information which often makes the difference between a successful subterfuge and an unsuccessful one. The person from whom you are seeking information should not only feel that no harm can come to the skip if he tells you what you want to know (or, better still, that the skip will feel a loss if he does *not* tell you), but also he should feel under pressure to part with the information right now. If you are to find out anything from these wary ones, you will be most successful if you can do it in one telephone call. By the time you call back a second time, your prospective informant may have talked with the skip and discovered that the skip had never known a "Biff" Davis in the Navy, had not lost a wallet, or had already received his W-2 form.

The relationship of the person you are questioning to the skip you are seeking should affect the role you adopt. If your prospective informant is a close relative or is apt to be in daily contact with the skip, the lost wallet strategem may be spotted as a hoax. Such a person could be in a position to know whether the debtor had experienced such a loss. On the other hand, an insurance investigator is more likely to make inquiries of those who know the skip well and are in frequent association with him.

The name you assume can help you if you are talking with some member of an identifiable group which could be expected to have a degree of solidarity. You might, for example, adopt an Irish name if the skip is Irish, or you could become Polish, Scotch or Armenian as convenient. You should not try to go too far in your efforts to identify yourself with such a group unless you really know what you are doing. It is very easy to make just a little slip which will give the game away.

Dangers of Subterfuge

The use of subterfuge has its dangers. No one likes to be tricked. If your deception is detected, your informant is apt to be angry and uncooperative. You may have lost all chance of getting information from that person. It is best to use the simpler and more straightforward methods unless it is absolutely necessary to resort to deception. The truth is easier to handle and, in all but the most difficult cases, it is just as effective. By and large, an honest approach which avoids deliberate deception will lead you to the kind of skips from whom you can collect after they have been located. Those who have taken elaborate precautions to prevent you from finding them will often go to equally great lengths to escape payment after they have been located, thus making your success of dubious economic value after it has been achieved.

Although it is recommended that you avoid deliberately misrepresenting yourself unless such appears unavoidable, you do not have to tell everything and put yourself at a disadvantage. There is a large area of honesty between being a blabbermouth and being deceitful. Your inquiries should be made circumspectly, at least.

Where to Look for the Skip

Whether you are candid or devious in your search for information about the location of the skip, you will obtain your leads from the information available to you on the credit application and the record of the account. Your analysis of this information may suggest some particularly promising beginning for your search, but usually one of the first sources of information to be explored is the place of employment.

Place of employment

You should call the debtor himself at his alleged place of employment. If he is there and you can talk with him, do so. Your search is ended. But, if you are told he is no longer in their employ, you should try to talk with the personnel manager or other person in charge of such matters as hiring and terminating. Inquire tactfully for their knowledge of the debtor. They may have information about where he is now working, or they may have a current address or telephone number. You should at least be able to find out what kind of work your skip did for them. If the employer should deny knowing where you could locate the debtor you might try asking where they sent or will send his W-2 form.

If you get inadequate information from the person in charge of personnel, it is sometimes a good idea to try to get in touch with the department in which your man worked. His former foreman or associates may have seen him on the street or have run into him elsewhere. They could know where he is employed at present. This is particularly true of salesmen. Salesmen keep unusually close track of one another and can often be of assistance. If the employer has a switchboard, do not forget to ask the switchboard operator. There is an outside chance that she might have a forwarding address or phone number.

Previous employers

You might also check with the debtor's previous employers. Even though the skip may not have been rehired, these previous employers may have received requests for references from the skip's current employer.

In making these inquiries and others, you will frequently be told that your respondent did not know the debtor very well. This is your cue for the magic question, "Who did know him?" Your question does not necessarily have to be couched exactly in these words, but you should avoid the negative form, "You don't happen to know the name of anybody who did know him better, do you?" But "Would you tell me the name of someone who did know him?" or even the simple demand, "Tell me the name of somebody who did know him," if spoken with the right inflection, are acceptable and effective forms. Always, though, try for a new lead, the name of another person whom you might question and who might know what you want to find out.

Trade references

Early in your tracing efforts you should check with any trade references you have on the debtor. Conduct the inquiry in the same manner in which you would handle a routine credit check. Be sure that you find out when the account with your reference was opened. If it was opened subsequent to the time you lost the debtor, you may have a good lead. If it should turn out that the reference is looking for your skip also, you may want to be frank about your purpose and combine efforts.

Personal references

If your inquiries of trade references fail to bear fruit, you may want to talk with the personal references if you have any. Here you have a difficult decision to make. Should you frankly state your purpose or should you pretend? There is no one answer which is best for all occasions. When in doubt, however, it is best to be frank. You do have a rather powerful argument of moral persuasion. You can appeal to the reference's integrity, by suggesting that he would not want his name to be used by someone else in an attempt to defraud a creditor. "Now, Mr. Doe, I am sure that a man of your standing would not want his name to be used to help someone cheat his creditors."

If, however, you feel uncertain of the reference's reaction to such an appeal, you might imply, without saying so, that you are a friend of the debtor. You would do this by adopting a casual and cordial tone, and you would use the debtor's first name when you speak of him. Whether you will want to drop the pretense or not depends upon your evaluation of the individual with whom you are speaking. If you feel that the reference is deliberately shielding the debtor, you may want to get off the line without revealing your purpose. If this is the case, it is possible, when the person whom you are questioning presses you too hard, to pretend a disconnect by flipping the receiver button and saying, "Hello, hello . . . darn it, I guess we got cut off," and at this point, of course, you hang up. Naturally the other person can hear you perfectly well, but you want him to think you cannot hear him.

Neighbors

By this time you may want to talk with neighbors of the skip. You can find the telephone numbers of neighbors by consulting a street address directory, often known as a criss-cross directory. Be discreet and tactful in your questions. You are imposing on these people and you should be grateful for their courtesy. Always thank them for their time, if not their help. Definitely, you want to find out from the neighbors the name of the landlord or real estate company which manages the property, whether or not the debtor has any friends in the neighborhood, and something of his habits. You might ask if they happen to know his employer or whether he drives a car. Although you will have to decide individual cases for yourself, it is usually best to be honest about your identity when you are asked directly. The times when your informant "clams up" in his desire to protect the debtor will be balanced by the times that he "opens up" to help you get to him.

Do not be so avid in your desire for specific information that you interrupt your informant. Some people are talkers and, if allowed to talk long enough, they will give you valuable information you would never have thought they had. When you have such a free-flowing talker on the line, it is often only necessary to signal that you are still listening with a "yes" or "uh-huh." Sometimes you can simply say, "You said . . ." and repeat part of one of the last sentences your informant uttered. This device will usually start a talker off again on another long dissertation. You may get much more information by allowing your informant to tell you what he knows in his own way than you would have gotten with factual questioning.

Landlord

Presumably you found out the name, and maybe the telephone number of the landlord when you checked with the debtor's neighbors. You would now check with the landlord. Usually real estate agencies have obtained bank references and employment before renting. You would like to know this information. They may also have a forwarding address or, at the least, can tell you when the debtor left the premises. You might use this date in checking with local moving and cartage concerns. These concerns might not only have a record of where the debtor moved *from* but would also know where they moved him *to*.

Credit bureau

Sometimes checking with the credit bureau will reveal information which will give you a start. At the worst you can usually find previous employers and previous addresses. Neighbors at former addresses may be better informed about the debtor's present whereabouts than those who lived near him at his last-known address. He may have lived at one of the previous addresses for a longer time or have had less reason to cover his tracks when he left.

Don't Forget His Family

Wife

The debtor has a family, as a rule. If he is married, consider what you know about his wife. In many cases, usually over 30 per cent, the wife will be working and may be easier to trace than the debtor. You would repeat the same steps with her employers that you used in your attempts to find the debtor himself. If you know that the debtor has been recently married, you can check with the marriage license bureau and get the maiden name of the wife. With this maiden name, you may be able to reach her relatives and they may know the location of the debtor. Again, you can go back and check with the credit bureau on her maiden name and, perhaps, uncover a whole new list of leads.

Children

If the debtor has children, and about 60 per cent of all households do, you may check with the superintendent of schools or with the principals of schools in those neighborhoods where the debtor might be located.

Relatives

In addition to his immediate family, you might have or have been able to obtain the names of other relatives. Your calls on relatives demand finesse. Although relatives may, quite understandably, be reluctant to help you, this is not always the case. Do not feel that you necessarily must resort to deception simply because the person you are calling is a relative. It sometimes happens that the debtor has alienated his relatives and they want to see someone catch up with him. More than one man has been "fingered" by an irate brother-in-law.

It is sometimes possible to locate relatives of the skip by calling persons with the same last name who have addresses in the vicinity of his last known address. Simply identify yourself by name, tell your respondent whom you are seeking, and state that he used to live at a certain address. Ask frankly if your respondent is a relative or knows the debtor. Sometimes the similarity in names leads to an acquaintance even when the skip is not a relative. Again, do not forget to be courteous and to close your inquiry with thanks.

Neighborhood businesses

Consider making inquiries of business people in the skip's former neighborhood. Do not forget the local grocery store or the local tavern. Bartenders often know more about their customers than the customers suspect. You may also bear in mind the possibility of checking with fuel dealers in the vicinity. Many renters have to provide their own coal or oil and may have accounts with fuel dealers nearby.

Janitors

In some cases it will be fruitful to try to get in touch with the janitor of the building. Be sure to ask the janitor the employment and the names of people who knew the debtor well. Depending on his degree of curiosity, he may be able to tell you a great deal about your debtor.

Telephone information

Of course, you should check with telephone information. Courtesy and persistence may persuade the information operator to be a real help. If your skip is located in a distant city and your community has direct-distance dialing, ask for information in the distant city. If you know an approximate address, the operator may know the city well enough to tell you whether there is a similar name nearby. If you get a telephone number, consider calling the debtor collect. It is often quite effective.

Tracing by Mail

All skip tracing is not done with the telephone. Indeed, some collectors think tracing by mail is more effective. Assuming that you have had mail returned, your first step is to examine the returned envelope closely. It will, of course, give a reason for return, but you can sometimes glean other valuable information from it. For example, "Refused" is quite a different reason from "Moved and left no forwarding address." The postal employee characteristically marks an envelope "not there," but the debtor who has received it and sends it back may mark it "not here." It will occasionally happen that a forwarding address has been marked on the envelope but the post office has not made an attempt to deliver it to the new address. You should examine the post marks. You will want to make sure that an attempt was made to deliver it, or send a new letter.

A number of sources of information are available to you through regular mail. All of those which were mentioned as being possibilities for telephone contact can also be reached by regular mail. Previous employers, neighbors, and references can all be reached with letters.

"Occupant"

The occupant of an address where the skip formerly lived may have the debtor's new address. If you cannot reach this occupant by telephone through the use of the street address directory, you may address a letter to "Occupant" at the address you have. As in most such requests for tracing information, you should include a stamped and self-addressed envelope to make reply easier and more probable.

Secretary of State

If you know or have reason to suspect that the skip owns an automobile, a letter to the Secretary of State or the Bureau of Motor Vehicles, depending on where such records are kept in your state, will get you information on the registration. More important, you will usually be able to get the identity of any lien holder on the automobile. The lien holder will quite often know where the debtor may be found. There is usually a fee for this service.

Armed Forces

If your skip is in the Armed Forces, a request to the appropriate service in Washington will bring you information about his address. The addresses for such requests are:

For the Army:

Department of the Army
Adjutant General Division
Washington 25, D.C.
Attention: Records Division

For the Navy
and Marine Corps:

Department of the Navy
Bureau of Naval Personnel
Washington 25, D.C.

For the Air Force:

Department of the Air Force
Air Adjutant General
Fees and Document Section
AFCAG–65F
Headquarters USAF
Washington 25, D.C.

Do not forget to include a fee of one dollar with all such requests, payable to the appropriate department.

Town officials

If you have traced the skip to a small town, a friendly letter to the librarian or the City Clerk may bring you a helpful reply. You cannot expect, nor will you receive, this kind of help in larger communities. In small towns, too, you will occasionally get some help from the local freight agent or even the Chief of Police. If the debtor has had a rural box number, you will occasionally get assistance by addressing a letter to "Mail Carrier Route Such-and-Such" and asking him for information about the debtor on his route.

Utilities

There is an outside chance that an inquiry to the gas or electric company in the community may yield information. Some utilities are cooperative.

Another outside chance in a small community is the Commissioner of Elections. It is possible that your skip has registered to vote and that the Commissioner will give you his address.

Occupation

When you know the debtor's trade or profession, new avenues of approach are open to you. Some trades and professions require state licensing, and information about these licensees may be had from the Secretary of State. The following is a partial list of those professions for whom licenses are often required:

- Barbers
- Beauticians
- Cab Drivers
- Chiropractors
- Dentists
- Insurance Agents
- Lawyers
- Morticians
- Notaries Public
- Nurses
- Osteopaths
- Pharmacists
- Physicians
- Plumbers
- Podiatrists
- Teachers

In addition, cities may also license occupations. The City of Chicago, for example, requires licensing of contractors and stationary engineers.

If the debtor happens to be a farmer, you might think of the local seed store, general store or dairy as likely sources of information. Farmers usually have dealings with such organizations.

If the debtor's occupation is one which requires membership in a union, this is a possibility. Although unions, as well as lodges and clubs, are reluctant to give out information about their members, you may address a certified or registered letter to the debtor at the organization marked "Forward—Deliver to addressee only." Your return receipt, if the letter is delivered, will give you the address you are seeking if you provide for a return receipt.

For many professions, although you will not often have a professional person who is a skip, there are directories at the library. You will find directories containing the addresses of the executives and directors of corporations, physicians, teachers, psychologists, and others at the local library. These directories not only give addresses but also have brief biographies which should help you to locate such individuals.

The Value of Using Registered or Certified Mail

The use of registered and certified mail is a tool for the skip tracer. Certified mail costs less, but the post office does not maintain records on certified mail as it does on registered mail. Otherwise the services are very similar. You can mark your mail with almost any kind of reasonable directions and they will be followed. When you mark it with such directions as "Forward," "Deliver to Addressee Only," or "Show Address where Delivered," you automatically get a relatively inexpensive skip tracing service from the Post Office Department. It is also possible to mark your envelope "Return to sender if not delivered on first attempt." If the envelope comes back marked, "Not in during hours of delivery," you may have located your skip without letting him know that you have done so. This can be a distinct advantage.

Developing Your Own Sources

As a skip tracer, you should make it a habit, particularly if you are working in a smaller community, to read the obituaries, hospital notes, and traffic court reports in your local newspaper. It is surprising how many debtors or relatives of debtors show up in the columns. In the case of an obituary, you should check the probate court for an estate.

You should actively seek to develop your own informants. Cultivate friendly relationships with people who are in a position to know about others. Such persons include bartenders, waitresses, union officials, personnel men, police officials, hospital administrators, city officials, and, indeed, almost anyone who deals with the public. If you are working in a smaller community, such contacts can become your very best skip-tracing resource.

You should not forget that you are seeking the debtor for a very definite purpose. It is not all merely an exercise in clever detective work. You want to collect money from him after you find him. In your inquiries, therefore, you will be alertly interested in finding out also where he works, where he banks, and the location and nature of any other financial resources he may have. Perhaps it will be simple to collect from the forgetful skip after you have him located, but the intentional skip can cause you as much trouble in the process of collecting as he did in locating.

If you are dealing with such an intentional skip, you should pursue your inquiry, after you have found him, into such matters as his income and resources. You would, of course, want to get this information before he was aware that he had been found. If you let him know before you are ready with enough information to force payment, he may skip again.

You may find it helpful in early attempts at skip tracing to refer often to the Skip Tracing Check List which follows for ideas. It is one way to be thorough and to be sure that you have not missed any of the more obvious sources of information. Ideally, though, you would pick up other leads as you check these out. You should write them down so that you don't forget them.

Skip Tracing Check List

General

1. Present employer
2. Former employers
3. Trade references
4. Neighbors
5. Landlord
6. Bank
7. Personal references
8. Relatives
9. Credit bureau
10. Local businesses

Clues and Hints

Janitor at residence? . . . Switchboard operator at employer? . . . Auto registration? . . . Children? Schools? . . . Occupation license? . . . Public utilties? Gas? Electric? Water? . . . Information operator? . . . Fuel dealers? . . . Newspaper circulation department? . . . Dog license? . . . Credit union? . . . Marriage license? . . . Filling station in neighborhood? . . . Mail carrier? . . . City Clerk? . . . Commissioner of Elections? . . . Librarian? . . . Trade union? . . . Club or lodge? . . . Grocery store? . . . Tap room? . . . Friends at previous employer? . . . Police records? . . . Maiden name of wife? Her relatives? . . . Moving and cartage companies? . . . Occupants of previous address? . . . Directories? . . . Armed Forces inquiry?

LOOKING FORWARD

XV

LOOKING FORWARD

With the expansion of consumer credit, it is inevitable that the absolute number of dollars lost as a result of non-payment will also rise. As this loss mounts there must be an increased awareness of the need for means of enforcing payment. Public sentiment, which was legitimately revolted by the abuses resulting from the old maxim, "Let the buyer beware," has swung to an extreme in order to protect the buyer. It must now moderate itself again to give some protection to the seller and to itself. After all, the public is the ultimate victim of those who fail to honor their contracts. The consumer pays in higher prices for the credit losses caused by the few who abuse the trust of credit.

Although it is true that some persons are victims of unscrupulous credit practices, current public opinion is often indiscriminately on the side of the debtor regardless of the merits of the case. The creditor and the bill collector are rather uniformly the villains of the piece. Rarely is one asked to consider the pathos of the man who has invested his savings in a business only to have it fail as a result of his misguided faith in the good intentions of his customers. On the other hand, articulate spokesmen are not often wanting for the debtor who, through his own actions, faces financial problems. The same persons who would be outraged by the blatant theft of merchandise side with those who steal through the abuse of trust.

In the midst of record personal incomes and an unprecedented prosperity, credit men are worried about the increasing numbers of personal bankruptcies. The attitudes of the public toward their financial obligations seem to be suffering a progressive deterioration, becoming more and more indifferent. The number of credit frauds seems to be on the rise.

Our highly developed use of consumer credit is one of the most important factors responsible for the expansion of our economy and this prosperity which we enjoy. Credit, however, rests on the institution of contract. Credit expansion cannot continue in a situation of gradual erosion of those forces which maintain this institution. Law and public sentiment must uphold the seller's right to collect his just debts.

Collection must become a respectable activity in the eyes of both the law and the public. If both continue to shelter the credit criminal we can expect the proportion of bad debt loss to rise. If such a rise continues unchecked, the cost of credit to the responsible buyer will eventually become prohibitive and consumer credit will contract.

Credit granters, in all their relations with the public, should try to get this message across. It is imperative that contracts be honored and that debts be paid. They should actively oppose legislation which encourages the irresponsible use of credit, and they should be articulate in defending their right for payment.

INDEX

T

Study Guide to Accompany

Maternal & Child Health Nursing

CARE OF THE CHILDBEARING & CHILDREARING FAMILY

FIFTH EDITION